A
Life
In
Hand

~

Creating
the
Illuminated
Journal

~

BY HANNAH HINCHMAN

PEREGRINE SMITH BOOKS

SALT LAKE CITY, UTAH

First Edition
95 94 93 92 91 5 4 3 2
Copyright © 1991 by Hannah Hinchman

Published by Gibbs Smith, Publisher
Peregrine Smith Books, P.O. Box 667, Layton, Utah 84041
(801) 544-9800

Design & Typography by Lee Riddell, Riddell Advertising & Design
Printed by Publishers Press on recycled paper

When ordering *A Life in Hand* with its companion blank book
in a boxed set, please use ISBN 0-87905-371-2

Library of Congress Cataloging-in-Publication Data
Hinchman, Hannah.
    A life in hand: creating the illuminated journal / Hannah Hinchman
        p.   cm.
    ISBN 0-87905-380-1 (pbk.) : $14.95
    1. Diaries – Authorship. 2. Illustration of books. I. Title.
PN4390.H5   1991
808.06692 – dc20   91-12329
                                                               CIP

This book is for my mother, and for Ruth Limmer

ACKNOWLEDGMENTS

Small and slight as it is, this book took a long time to complete. Several people deserve thanks for urging and coddling it and me. Joan Hamilton, editor at *Sierra,* invited me to write the article on which this book is based. Gibbs Smith had the vision for the book, and Heather Bennett carefully guided it along. Michael Kenney gave me lots of time and space to brood, pull dozens of books off the shelves and throw papers all over the floor. Dr. David Love restored me to confidence repeatedly with his never-failing faith in this project. Clare Walker Leslie commiserated and advised as a devoted student of journal keeping. When I believed that my true vocation might be rewinding typewriter correction ribbons, Tex Garry, Anna Moscicki, Tim Sandlin, Geoff O'Gara and Berthenia Crocker, my brother Lew and his wife Sandy, ignored me and asked how the book was coming. Bless Laurie Gunst for the many evening discussions that reestablished the splendor of the world. And bless Bruce Cameron for jumping into the vision and helping me keep sight of it.

Lee Riddell's sensitive and informed design ideas made this a beautiful book. Of course my mother is the one who started me on this path by her encouragement and the example she set all through my childhood of the mom-at-the-typewriter who I was proud not to disturb. I can't express my gratitude to Ruth Limmer for making me understand what writing is about; I wish everyone could have a teacher like her.

And thanks to my trusty horse Scout who carried me safely for many a daydreaming, sky-gazing mile.

leven years ago I was only erratically faithful to the journal I kept in a frayed spiral notebook, pouncing on it with passionate fervor for a few weeks and then disdaining for months the daub of my lefthanded crab-scrawl. But if there is a notebook somewhere that records my thoughts that spring as I considered whether or not to move from Washington, D.C., to Wyoming, it surely mentions my first encounter with Hannah Hinchman.

Somewhere in the old files at *High Country News* you could find the critique I wrote of that Wyoming publication, trying to convince them I could make a difference there as an editor. I swung my saber at their news reporting and catapulted their opinion pieces over the wall, but put roses at the feet of a small column in *HCN* called "Afield."

That was Hannah's column, a modest record of Wyoming observations. A dipper singing in the water, the green rosettes of dandelions, followed by: "Each year spring undoes me more completely." A line drawing only two inches wide of sand dunes, river, and full moon; a denser rendering of the dandelion itself. I had never been to her part of Wyoming. But here was the smell and taste of a place, poised . . .

For a professional writer, journal-keeping is mercenary. I have tried at times to work through my problems by consulting myself in writing, and I've tried to regularize my life with a morning tea-cup of record-keeping, but it never works. My journal always resorts to cold-eyed thievery. It thrives inversely to the writing I do for public consumption. I turn to it during fallow periods, and it fills up like water rising in a canal lock; when a kind of equilibrium is reached, the gates open and I turn to an article or a short story; I pick through the journal, steal from it, and otherwise shun it.

I have felt the fragile, private pages of Hannah's journals under my fingers and stood in a crowd admiring her interplay of image and word hanging on a gallery wall. I don't ever expect the words I write in a journal to follow the contour of badlands across the page in readable script, or to

5:00 a.m. — camp on Soda Fork. Fannie Mae waits to be packed.

emerge from the mouth of a finely rendered blackbird. But for practical reasons, I'm trying to loosen up: now and then a stem of ragweed is crudely etched across a notebook page — how else will I ever identify what I can't name on the spot?

As you will learn from this book, there are as many ways of keeping a journal as there are people. If someone shares their journal, accept its limitations with gratitude. I've recently been going through the journals of a great-great aunt that were sent to me by her granddaughter. This woman lived in California late in the nineteenth century. She recounts no dialogue, tells me nothing about what they ate or wore, won't even give me a weather report. But I can feel the anxiety in her terse accounts of the ore her husband brought daily down the mountain from their failing gold mine. That is the fragment my imagination needs. She has opened a door in time. Just as Hannah, years ago, opened a door to Wyoming.

Her own art has evolved, and today Hannah might find those journals from the 1970s too cramped, even a little precious. Today, her drawing hand is freespending. The color is braver. Beneath the stones she turns in a Wyoming streambed she may find Joyce or Colette. She needs large pages, more freedom to describe. A dozen springs have even more undone her.

But she will forgive the limitations of her earlier journals, just as she is generous now in praising those who went

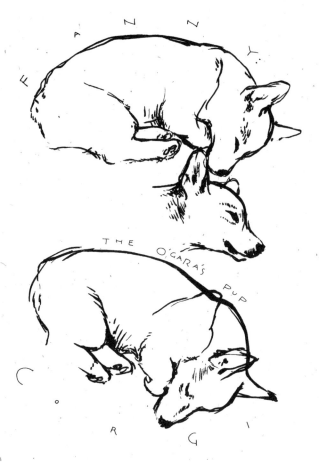

before, and encouraging those who follow. Doors open on a world, and then you find another door. When he was quite old, E.B.White wrote: "Even now, this late in the day, a blank sheet of paper holds the greatest excitement there is for me — more promising than a silver cloud, and prettier than a red wagon."

— *Geoff O'Gara*

TOOLS OF MEMORY & IMAGINATION

ost of us, sorting through childhood memories, have remarked that it isn't always the significant event or the important day we remember. It is more likely to be an apparently random detail, like the pattern on a dress our mother wore, or the smell of dust on a hot street when the first drops of rain hit it. Even though we don't remember who came to our fourth birthday party, we probably have a vivid recollection from childhood of how the seasons felt; exactly how cool the air was in the summer shade as we drank a glass of cold lemonade. The apparently random details cohere. They form memories that are distinct, unique and eternally fresh.

What is it about the child's mind that allows it to register impressions with such clarity? We know the child hasn't a more sophisticated way of gathering information; it's the same fluid, haphazard process we use as adults. But our receptivity diminishes as we mature; we must channelize our lives to get along in the adult world.

levi

polly by the river

levi's shell

Before that channelizing begins, the child can linger in self-forgetfulness. She stands and gazes or listens, and lives in the gazing or listening. There is nothing held back, she is all eyes and ears. Nor is she projecting anything, not generalizing or classifying. She's being impressed.

How to invite that immersion, how to arrive at it more readily? We recognize Thoreau's keen eye. A meadow, far from being undifferentiated green, was to him an intricate profusion of specific plants and creatures whose forms, colors, and habits he knew well. Thoreau and the other great naturalists were almost invariably journal keepers. Most great writers are journal keepers — it's where writing becomes second nature to them. We know the great artists through their finished paintings, but their sketchbooks reveal a roving, observant eye through which they gathered knowledge about how the world is put together.

They all discovered a simple but highly effective tool for deepening perception. They made records of what they observed — written or drawn — or both.

Two incidents sum up for me the little-known rewards of keeping a journal. Once, two friends and I made a camp in a wide mountain meadow beside a river in Wyoming. The first morning I awoke knowing that my only task that day was to explore and appreciate where we were.

I sat in the doorway of the tent and opened my journal, beginning to draw whatever caught my eye. A foot away were mountain bluebells still dew-heavy. I tried to draw the shapes of their bent bells, swaying like hoop skirts. I drew the pancakes in the skillet on the campfire, the blackened coffeepot, the smooth stones around the coals. I drew the saddles and their blankets laid out neatly on a log, drew the horses and mules drifting up a hillside through bluebells.

While drawing, I made notes of our sparse morning conversation and of the other sounds I was hearing: hermit thrushes singing from the deeper forest and bells around the horses' necks. Wandering a little further afield, I drew a variety of wildflowers, identifying some and making notes on others; and I diagramed the way streams threaded through the meadow.

What I had done, opening the journal, was to open a door, or more truthfully, to become a door. Images and events passed through me to settle on the pages. I was as completely absorbed and attentive as I am able to be. It might have been easier to have eaten my pancakes while I looked around, but I would never have come away with such an indelible impression of the meadow. I also wound up with a tangible record, now a treasure to me.

The other incident is of a very different nature. When I turned thirty, it happened that many other rough things converged on top of that birthday, traumatic enough by itself. In my second year of art school, suddenly the lights went out. There seemed no avenue of change; I couldn't imagine one. Day

after day I made the same stiff
drawings. Paints became inert
sludge on my brush. My husband,
insulated in his successful
career, seemed far away.
Either I couldn't express
my despair well
enough, or he didn't
want to hear about it.

I alternated between
overwhelming sleepiness and nervous energy ready to
ignite into rage. Looking through my journal at that time I
see cramped or half-finished drawings, falsely cheery
entries about the weather, then long feverish, almost
surreal passages about what I was reading, seeing and
thinking. Not much about what I was feeling; perhaps
because I wasn't. Lots of cryptic morning-after entries of
contrition for having lost my temper or otherwise ruined an
evening with my husband, or with friends, when this
aimless, hopeless anger got hold of me.

Then a change began to occur. When my little cat died, I
hit bottom, and from there I must have known a last-ditch
effort was required to survive. The drawings disappeared
and my handwriting changed from precise and miniature to
sprawling and hurried. I launched into entries that take on
the very heart and structure of my life, harrowing and
merciless, some of them. But the journal was the ideal

listener. It stood aside and allowed many selves to speak without getting confused, impatient or judgmental.

Then suddenly brush drawings of chrysanthemums erupted into the pages. There are entries about moving, making new schedules, conversations with friends. At the time I was just doing my best to get from day to day; now I see the outline of a powerful process of healing, outwitting or outwaiting darkness and being restored to health. The journal, so compact and so humble, is vast and can contain whole lives.

LIFE IN HAND

Most of us, normal people who aren't astronauts or living in a country undergoing revolution, probably see our lives as unworthy of careful observation. Quite the opposite is true. Each of us is supplied with the same basic equipment as the first human, and lives under the conditions that make being human so remarkable: we have an arsenal of senses, in a world of countless things to sense. We have minds that can hold images and form ideas of past, present and future all at once. We have won a moment in the unfolding universe. Doesn't that warrant comment?

Journal keeping is as old as our ability to think of ourselves as unique individuals. A book has always been at hand to record journeys, epic events. The traveler and the witness know that their moment in history is singular and feel the need to preserve an account of it. The long poem-songs memorized and retold through history are the fruits of that impulse. The great naturalists, aware of their privileged positions, turned keen eyes on a new continent, wanting to capture that never-to-be-repeated moment.

The kind of journal I want to talk about in this book is an inclusive kind, one that maps actual or inner places, that can be used for things as diverse as recipes or soul-searching inner dialogues. It can be a place to deposit anger, or a place to sketch floorplan after floorplan for your dream house. The juxtaposition of such apparently unrelated parts of your life may seem strange at first; your

narcissi · march 6

sense of order may object to it. Try to resist that voice.

It's just those juxtapositions, in fact, that generate some of the best journal results. The little sketch you did one morning of the way people ran for shelter from a brief downpour might end up seeming oddly (or mysteriously) related to your entry on the other side of the page about the work and home pressures you were feeling at the time. The journal has a way of making unexpected con- nections like that. Some of them are just funny, some are illuminating. They remind you that your life is not just an aimless drifting string of days, but something purposeful, with distinctive traits and cycles, many of which you may know little about. Journal keeping can sometimes bring them to light, revealing the outline of your own life.

WHY BEGIN?

What prompts the urge to keep a journal? Some start theirs in adolescence, when everyone needs a way to establish a separate identity. Others, in an adult crisis, find they need a way to write out their anguish, anger, confusion. Some, like me, hope to preserve chunks of new knowledge; the names of plants and animals in my native Ohio fields seemed like the key to a new life for me — and were.

Others begin a journal as an assignment for a class or in counseling. Some begin one when they have a child, because they have a new reason to see significance in the present. Some begin one as a place to copy and store articles, poems, quotations — gathering pieces to form a coherent world view. Many begin when they feel their' lives accelerating and slipping away; they have a vague sadness that so much seems lost. They sense that they aren't deeply affected by things, and don't remember enough. They want a deeper connection to the world.

Is there an ideal time to begin a journal? A person at fifty-five may be in the midst of profound life changes, but thinks it's too late to start one, that it wouldn't make any sense because so much of his/her life has elapsed. But it doesn't work that way. When you begin a journal, it's like arriving at a mountain pass. Even  though it has taken you days to get there, as you look back, the whole route is open to your inspection. Facing ahead, you're in a good position to look at the country

something about
the way the
April blizzard
light comes
in the HCN
window.........

My space up
under the eaves...
As I'm drawing, nuthatches
are pecking the logs outside...

before you, and choose possible routes from there.

The tools of memory and imagination acquire new power when they go to work in the journal. Most of us have a stock collection of stories that we repeat to ourselves and others, without bothering to reexamine them. We call those stories memories, but surely there's more to our pasts than just these few snapshot tales. There is always the urge to doctor memories, to turn them into causes or justifications for a current self-interpretation. The journal is, as I have learned from my own experience and from talking to many other journal keepers, a remarkable way to recover truths about your past.

It's not necessarily true that the best time to write about your past is when you are young and the incidents are still recent. The poet Louise Bogan was of the opinion that "the best time to write about one's childhood is in the early thirties, when the contrast between early forced passivity and later freedom is marked; and one's energy is in full flood." She did her first round of reexamining the past in her thirties, and took it up again in her fifties, when she found "the final antidote: to love and forgive."

WHEN TO BEGIN

The best time to begin keeping a journal is whenever you decide to. My first volumes's title page is inscribed July 24, 1970. Not a day of any significance at all except that I was in the midst of the first summer that I had ever really seen. The accumulated need to preserve some of it was answered when the book came into my hands.

The real magic wrought by the journal goes beyond the excitement you feel choosing things to go on the first few pages. It begins to show up subtly as you notice you are about to close the cover on a first complete volume. You look back through it, picking out the small developments, the highs and lows. You reread a long late-night dialogue, and notice how the flavor of one day seemed to sum up a whole season. Patterns float to the surface. You realize that when you began the journal you were drifting along, following your routines, but one day had been much like others before it. Now as you look through these pages distinctions become clear, you see evidence that the journal is an instrument that brings your life into sharper focus.

Working in the journal, you try to choose vivid particulars, you reach for the ability to capture "the undying difference in the corner of a field." The writing has become more incisive — possibly also more abrupt and awkward, but less laden with the cliches and automatic phrases that probably filled the first pages. Your drawings no longer look like attempts to copy someone else's style. Now they are unpredictable and some of them are ugly, but they are an authentic record of what you beheld, a real effort to get beyond the superficial.

I hope that the blank book you buy with this book will suit you. Try to select a paper that is heavy enough to handle vigorous drawing, and smooth enough to allow most pens to move over it easily. Art supply stores and some enlightened book stores carry them. Don't start with the most beautiful and expensive volume, just get a sturdy well-bound artist's sketchbook. Resist the urge to buy the nicely bound books with lined pages. They look appealing, but they have a deadening influence: too much like the paper we wrote on in school and too dictatorial in forcing us to write on equally spaced lines. And of course you can't draw on

Still trying to fit in square basket

lined pages. To me, a journal doesn't reach its full potential until you are both drawing and writing in it, switching from one to the other with ease.

Avoid at all costs those "theme" journals with decorations and little sayings already plugged into the pages. Don't they contradict all the reasons for keeping a journal? They carry a built-in insult: the assumption that you can't do it yourself. If you can't find a hardbound book, or a sewn paperback, get a sturdy spiral-bound sketchbook. Page size doesn't matter, you'll adjust to whatever size you have.

A small book is more convenient to carry, an advantage at first as you try to establish the habit, and less conspicuous to open in public. There are available handy nylon covers that have various pockets; one of those could allow you to include the journal as part of a traveling office.

Just begin. Any day, any moment. There need be no occasion, no noteworthy event. Think of your beginning as the point where a tossed pebble hits the surface of a pond. Changes and discoveries will widen out endlessly from just such a small point. Take your life as it is, and go from there.

THE LITTLE
OAK TREE

FIVE ICE-BREAKING EXERCISES

like to make a title page for each new volume with the date and the volume number. Usually I include a quotation from a poem or piece of writing I like, as a talisman. Or I will choose words that mirror the tenor of my life at the moment, as well as I can understand it. I often include a dedication, to involve a person or people I love in the making of the book.

The title page can be beautifully decorated and illuminated. I relish the momentousness of starting fresh with a new book, but beginning can also be intimidating. One way to circumvent that is to open the book to the third or fourth or fifth page and start in with an entry there. That way the terror of facing the white expanse will be broken. The book will have been initiated in a casual offhand way that makes adding to it easier and removes some of the fear of designing a title page.

If you hope to be a long-time journal keeper you must strike a balance between momentousness and play. It helps to believe that the book is important and that what you put into it will be the most lively and articulate work you can produce. But you must allow the book to include lots of awkward first attempts, experiments, and just plain drivel. If you take it too seriously you'll write only dull, careful entries, and do only pale, safe drawings.

Here is a collection of ideas to help you get into the process of keeping a journal, and to give you a glimpse of how many different ways it can be done. They are good beginning exercises because they will throw you into drawing and writing at once, showing how one can urge and augment the other. They take liberties with the familiar narrative form that often restricts us. The exercises should be useful in opening the door to memory and imagination as well as getting you to observe and describe carefully. These five are useful for the veteran too, to break out of ruts and wake you up. Most people, unless they took courses that forced them to try different styles, have only one voice that emerges when they write. Receiving letters, I am usually disappointed because the actual person is so much more vivid than the one I meet on the page. The kind of writing that earned an *A* on a book report doesn't work very well as a vehicle to penetrate the life that lies in glory around you.

In school we are taught to make summations and state positions, not to write vividly about tangible things. Depriving writing of its richness so early does much to diminish our ability to see. I am disturbed that so many letters actually do read "How are you? I am fine." And we know the writer had to struggle for something to say beyond that. I would prefer to read "My nailpolish is chipped and the snow is melting" than something so dull as an average letter. What do we have that is utterly unique to us, after all, but these days, in these surroundings?

We need initially to strip away the tendency to generalize and explain (though we need those skills, too) and get back to the barest, plainest facts. Looked at with a discerning eye, a season, *spring,* turns out to have many seasons within it, many degrees of spring. The same is true for our lives, our surroundings. We can't see the stunning complexity and drama when we operate in broad, standard

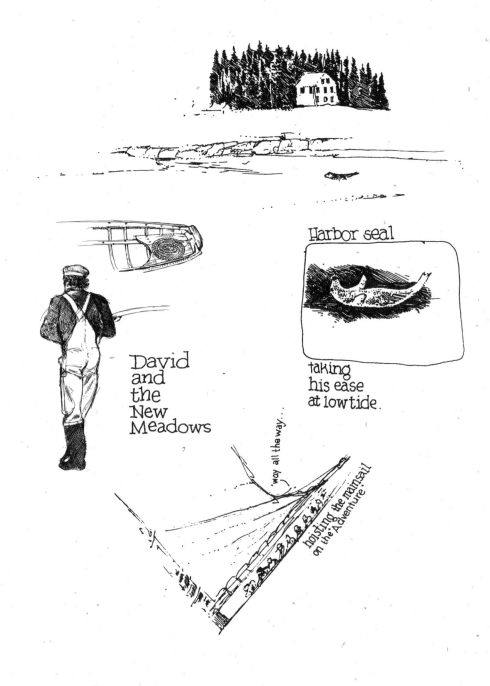

Harbor seal

taking
his ease
at low tide.

David
and
the
New
Meadows

"way all the way..."

hoisting the mainsail
on the 'Adventure'.

Coming out of Burnt Coat Cove

categories. One good way to elude the categories is to come face to face with the physical world.

Try any or all of these exercises.

1) FIELD OBSERVATION

Take your book and a pen that's comfortable for both writing and drawing and find an everyday, unarranged still life. It might be a workbench with tools out, left by someone in the middle of a project. Or, in the dish drainer you may find an array of dishes and utensils. Or shoes in the closet, things on your desk. Look for a few moments at the configuration. Then choose one of the elements, the one you want to start with.

With a very simple, childlike line, begin to shape the initial object you've chosen to draw. Don't try to be artistic and don't be faint-of-heart about your line. Be straight-forward and bold. The lines can overlap, they can stop and start over again, they can cover each other up in a way that comes from really looking, seeing amendments, trying new adjustments.

What you want is a quick and lean portrayal, but one that doesn't resort to abstraction. In other words, don't substitute a rectangular box for the dictionary on your desk. Look carefully at the dictionary and let your hand move around taking simple visual notes about the slant here and a bit of print on the cover, and those little half-moon page cuts that show you where to open for a particular letter.

You want the personality of the dictionary, if possible.

After you have spent about ten minutes getting some lines down from the first item of your still life, launch out and make something like a map to show the positions of the other elements in it. Just a small place-holding mark will do, or a corner, a curve, an intersection. Go ahead and let the drawing spill across both pages of the book as much as it needs to. Your position map will let you go on drawing the other objects without being distressed, finding you've put them in the "wrong" places. It will show you how much space your drawing is going to take up, so you won't end up cramming everything on one page.

After you've given ten minutes to the position map, go further into the drawing taking another fifteen minutes or so. There's no need to include everything you see, or give it all equal attention. Edit out objects wherever you want, and linger over the things that most interest you. Keep your approach and attitude simple. Instead of thinking "I must render this realistically, using shading and getting all the proportions right," say, "Look how that dark spot sits right next to that light place, and how those pages curl up on the ends as if they've been used over and over."

When the time is up, put the pen down and look over the arrangement again. How much more about it do you know now than you did before you started to draw? As you look back at your drawing, choose a piece of white space anywhere on the two pages. Inside the drawing or out, it

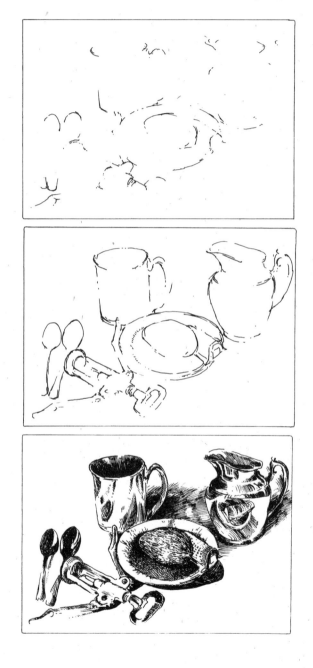

doesn't matter. Pick an appealing space and give a very specific but very lean description of what you just drew, about thirty words or so. You don't need to describe it in any clever or poetic way. The purpose is to clear away the fog and just see the things themselves. Don't worry about sentence structure or correct grammar at this point. This is to be a pared-down description, analogous to the line drawings you just finished.

For instance, I see on my desk a "silver cream pitcher, curved near the neck, beside a plate holding avocado and nutmeg grater. Silver surface has accurate but bent reflections of things around it."

That's enough to let me feel that I have had a good look at the bowl and gotten down something useful about it. Not an exhaustive catalog, not a poetic expression, just field notes. It's actually harder than you might think to give a plain but specific description.

For this type of writing, which becomes one of the mainstays of the journal keeper, you'll find that much of the grammar required for formal writing can be left out, leaving very compressed information. Thus, "my black cat has just come in and gone to sleep inside the square wicker basket that holds my letter paper and envelopes" can become, "black cat in, asleep in square wicker basket on letter paper, envelopes." Though it may seem insignificant in the example of one sentence, knowing that you can get a lot down with a minimum expenditure of time and energy will make a difference in whether you open your book often or not. That kind of pared-down writing also helps to short-circuit thinking habits we acquired when learning formal writing.

Give yourself three minutes to fit a description into a piece of white space. Then try another one, totally different from the first — just to remind yourself that there is no single way to look at something.

One of the dangers of life without a journal is that we would have to entrust the events of our lives to memory alone. My memory is feeble and capricious, and the information it does store sometimes gets "corrected" by my ego. But if we are working toward the ideal of an examined life, we want to be able to know and understand our pasts, so we have to use whatever memories we can get hold of. For most of us, access to those musty storage aisles is the main problem. Instead, we repeat stories to ourselves in place of the actual living images, and risk missing the significance that still lies intact in the memories. We need to get into the raw data banks and look for new information.

Next, try a deceptively simple exercise that allows you to open a volume of memory and work with it for awhile. Approaching memory this way seems to work better than trying to isolate events or answer specific questions. It brings into focus more of the context, and that's where the train of associations appears.

2) MEMORY WALKING

Choose a place from your childhood. It can be your own backyard, or a local territory, or a field and woods you frequented. Or it can be the interior of a house or apartment you lived in or one you liked to visit. (This isn't intended to take you back to scenes of trauma or cataclysm, so try to choose a place with happy or neutral memories). Spend some time with your eyes closed, letting the image of the place become clearer.

Now, imagine you are walking there, or opening the front door and going inside. Let yourself remember very specific things, like the shape of the door handle or obstacles on the path. You will be amazed at the details your child mind stored away. Calling up those details is something your memory likes to do, and it will oblige then by delivering to you whole scenes and sequences you didn't realize were in there.

As you did in the first exercise, look around without being analytical. Don't concentrate on the exact dimensions of

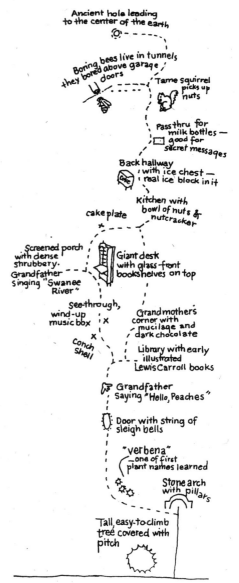

the room or the number of acres in the field. What were
your landmarks? What was your route? What places did
you like to return to? When you feel that you are
back in the place, turn to your book and start
a simple map of it, allowing a full two-page
spread for it.

This map is not intended to be a
drawing, and not even a bird's eye
view of anything. Make the map
as though you were touring or
walking through the place,
perhaps just a simple winding
line with marks along it. Close
your eyes again and start at the beginning. When you
come to the first site you want to transcribe (it could be
where the houses stopped and the woods began, or it could
be the shape of the door handle), make a mark on the map
and begin a description, closing your eyes whenever you
want to allow yourself to see the place again.

Do you feel your child viewpoint returning? What you as
an adult could describe now as an armoire, your child eyes
would see as "a big wooden thing with clothes hanging
inside." That's what you want, let that voice have a chance
to speak up. Open up all the sensory avenues. How did
the fringe on the upholstery feel? How did the crushed
acorns smell? Go from room to room, or around the
territory, noticing things and putting them down on the

map as they appear to you, using the pared-down style we just experimented with. You don't want to be encumbered by grammatical niceties as you work to transcribe elusive images in your memory.

Your descriptions will probably not reflect the overall picture that an adult would register, but rather things significant to the child that you were. When I did this exercise once, I recalled an unexplained hole in my grandmother's backyard. It was a site of mystery to me: I thought it went to the center of the earth and was made by prehistoric people. Revisiting it in my memory I realized that it was nothing more than the hole meant to hold the shaft for the clothesline. That impressed upon me how much drama children invest in the world, and how impoverished we are living solely in a place where holes all

have explanations. Learning the reason for that hole, though, did nothing to diminish the child-sensation that is preserved intact, full of intrigue in my memory, and now in my journal.

Still, while you are there, keep your adult eye roving. You may gain insight into the kind of person you were then. In that same exercise, walking through my grandmother's house, the images showed me that I was

often alone, and a little lonely and aimless, or dreamy. I
was not a child out drumming up activities or exploring a
wider territory. That was a valuable piece of knowledge; I
no longer feel so compelled to change the solitary and
lonely aspect of my personality. I see it has been with me
from the beginning, and is sometimes a source of strength.

There may of course be people and animals in the place
you revisit, but for this exercise try not to let them divert

you. There is much more emotional freight involved in encounters with people and animals, and that makes it harder to bring images into focus, which is what we want to do here. When you have that skill, then it will be time to return and meet those characters again.

Include as many or as few items as you wish. This exercise can carry you away, and you may want to write pages and pages, one thing leading into the next, so many vivid details, and insights into the self you were then. If you have all night, go ahead. If you want a limit, give yourself an hour.

Most of us have trouble just sitting and thinking. Many times I have heard people say that they have some of their best ideas while they are knitting or walking or driving. If we try to sit and think we get fidgety; nervous energy makes us want to tap our finger, scratch an itch, or get up and pace. Buddhists and practitioners of yoga have made it their goal to get past the needlings of nervous energy to a deeper layer of stillness. Drawing involves a different kind of concentration than what is experienced during meditation, but it diverts nervous energy, allowing the mind to roam and range in freedom. Following is an exercise that uses drawing as a meditative tool, to be combined with writing. In the process of journal keeping we need time to sort thoughts, to allow things to surface in our minds. Drawing is the ideal way to spend those moments.

3) MEDITATIVE SKETCHING

Choose something to draw that is complex enough to challenge you, but not so intricate that you'll be baffled getting all its parts arranged. Start with a quick position map, in pencil, laying in the general areas in much the same way you did in exercise 1. Then, settle in with the drawing with pen or pencil, content to work on an area until you get it to just the right level of gray or black.

Surprisingly, I do some of my best drawing when my thoughts are roaming, when I am only intermittently paying close attention to the drawing and deciding to change or add things. Many times a drawing will involve a large dark expanse, or several chunks of black and a variety of grays. Too often people begin drawings with a lot of creative zest, but when it comes to really putting in the time that the drawing requires, executing those blacks and grays, they get impatient. If you relax and decide that in the course of completing this exercise you will give the drawing plenty of time and patience, you'll probably end up pleased with what you've drawn. Of course not all drawings need to be finished to the degree I describe here, but some do. If you take the work of drawing, much of it rhythmical and repetitive, like weaving, and combine it with directed thought, the result is a fruitful and satisfying process.

If you work in pencil, it's best to have several, some that are hard (identified by an H, as in 4H) and some that are

The Warm Sooty Coat Corner

soft (identified by a B, as in 6B)   The harder pencils will make smooth gray tones, the softer ones will make rich dark grays and blacks. If you work in pen or marker, grays will be achieved by a loose weave of dots or strokes. Make the weave denser as you move toward black.

While your hands and eyes are busy drawing, let your mind settle on these questions: How can I describe the atmosphere, character, or trend of the day, from its beginning?   The past week?   My overall life at this juncture? Answers should include both outer and inner experiences, noting especially where they have affected each other. As you go over these questions, stop the drawing whenever you hit on a key image or idea and in the very briefest way, perhaps only half a dozen words, make a little note below the drawing.

An entry describing the week might sound like this: "Watching for returning birds. Sound of bluebird notes in incessant wind. Doing mental stuff in A.M., physical in P.M., not usual pattern. Sleep without dreams. Resilient against bad weather. Realize that D.R. is not what I thought he was. Firewood low." The comments may not seem to go together, but who says they have to? With a set of notes like this you are prepared to tackle a longer, more discursive entry when you have given the drawing about half an hour.

The next part of the exercise invites a more reflective writing style than the bare-bones notes you used above. The main thing to bring from the notes is an appreciation for the telling detail. When you begin writing here, resist the urge to go back to generalities like, "This has been a pretty happy spring for me. I've done a lot of interesting things and read some good books." What will that tell you ten years from now? How much will you really be discovering as you write an entry like that? Reach for comparisons, turning points, bits of conversations, actual moments that stick in your mind and what you were thinking at the time.

Here is a brief passage from Colette, the French writer, who was one of the greatest of journal keepers. See how she fills her sentences full of telling detail.

"I record here, with respect, one of the last poses of this great tragic actress, [Sarah Bernhardt] then about to reach her eightieth year: the delicate and withered hand offering the brimming cup, the flowery azure of the eyes, so young still in their network of fine lines, the questioning and mocking coquetry of the tilted head, and that indestructible desire to charm, to charm still, to charm right up to the gates of death itself."

A beetle hurrying to cross the drive.

When I touch him with my boot he up-ends as if to stick his head in the sand. (But he intends to squirt me)

This fellow a casualty too— fell intact out of the sky.

...another casualty very much expanded Siamese cat.

As you write you will become aware that thought moves in an ebb-and-flow rhythm. You will have a flash of thought, and turn to write it out. After that there will be a period of re-forming. Let the notes you took while drawing prompt your next passage, or read back through what you've just written, to see if a sentence two paragraphs back contained another idea that you passed by at the time. At first an idea may appear briefly and vaguely, it vanishes too fast for you to trace it. But the practice of journal keeping will improve your ability to generate ideas and get them down quickly, so don't despair if it seems hard at first. If you feel truly stuck, take up the drawing again; give your mind more time to organize and respond.

Finally we come to a halt on a forest road near the lake ∼ crawl in the
back — heat, mosquitos, worry — and W. doesn't sleep much. Take off again,
H. drowsing & dreaming in the back, W. with second wind, singing &
covering ground. Dark ∼ concentrated lake sunset in storm & murk. Later
H. takes the wheel through Wisconsin forests (on the cross-state route 8)
Maybe in was just pre-dawn rapture but remember the forests in
headlight gusts, leaf silversides, fir diagonals, deep forest pressing in all
around. With deer & other animal eyes lighting up. Powdermilk
biscuit land. Our great find: Audrey's Spot Café, open till 2:00 A.M,
in downtown Ladysmith, Wisconsin. Few middle age honky tonkin
couples winding down with good coffee & pie from Audrey's.
  Overheard in Lobby of Sheridan Inn: "She was just heartsick
over what they were doing to the land, tearing it up." "But you

Know its true, look at what happened with the Tucker Ranch...

Narrative will continue but this day — essentially a fixture on the grand veranda of the Sheridan Inn — reading an issue of "Montana History" about women in the wilderness, drawing & writing. Wendell returns every now & again from Law firm interviews. Just now tired of the hard chairs on the porch & so moved inside to the Saloon, 40¢ drafts, a grand & ornate wooden bar with beveled glass mirrors. My little table looks to be made of real wood, old, & the chairs are exactly the same as my beloved little oak chair from Lander. The generous rooms in this Hotel are painted (surfaces not woodwork) a deep vermilion, lovely. Unlike bars in Maine where conversations seem closed & people posture & ogle, the small groups here are buckling down to the bar, animated, open & friendly.

Try not to be too self-critical. If an attempt to capture the current flavor of your life becomes a list of complaints and faults and judgments, you've missed the point. Ask questions instead. That is much less likely to dry up the flow of thought. Allow yourself at least an hour for the whole exercise.

at the
DENVER
BOTANIC
GARDENS

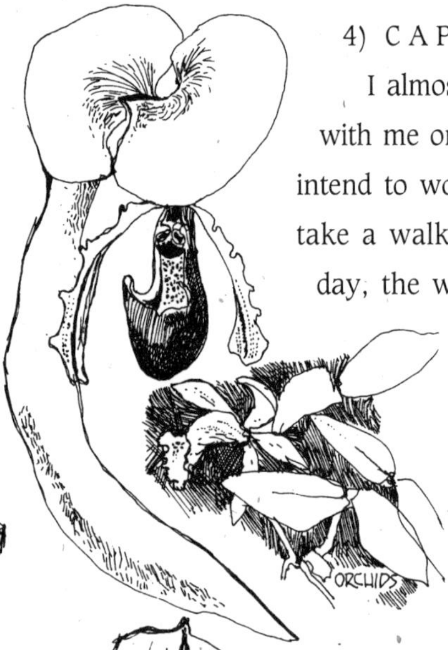

ORCHIDS

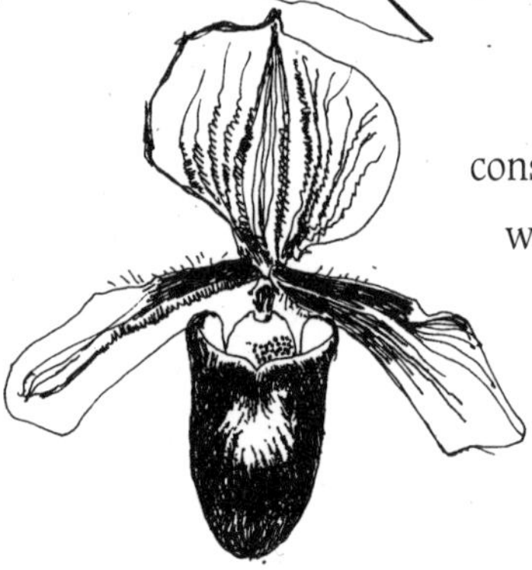

4) CAPTURE THE DAY

I almost always have my journal with me on long excursions. But if I intend to work in it at home, I like to take a walk to get in touch with the day, the weather, the activity of the creatures that live around me. No matter if I'm out fifteen minutes or two hours, I always come back with things to report and things to draw. I walk with as much attention as I can muster, constantly framing questions: exactly what colors of twigs are there in this willow clump? What kind of track is that and what was the animal doing? I see this drift is melting—where is it melting fastest? How does the snow change as it melts?

I always try to read the clouds — I'm usually wrong in my projections — but I am at least noticing the different kinds of clouds and what they are doing, searching for words that might get down their true nature (or as close as words can get to that.)

If I have time I will follow tracks, or dig around in vole runways, or wait for the hawk to come back over the hill. Finding the correct answers to my questions is not my sole aim, however. Like Thoreau, I've learned that the answer might not show up for years, or never. So I don't get frustrated not knowing. I'll note, and perhaps draw a flower then some other time get out the field guides and look it up, checking on other accumulated questions and other flowers more intensively. The point is that looking at the thing is more important than knowing its name.

tree sparrows waiting

Go for a walk. If you can, take one that will keep you outside long enough to pass over what I call the *color threshold.* In the early stages of a walk, for some reason, colors seem only pleasant and ordinary. If I am outdoors long enough, usually an hour or more, all the colors begin to become more brilliant and distinct. Color combinations I wouldn't have noticed at first become striking. Could it be because of the influx of oxygen and blood to the brain? Is it the effect of the outdoor light saturating the color receptors in the eye? I don't know, but I am always happy when I notice it happening.

Try to stay as watchful as a coyote for the duration of the walk. Even if you find yourself taking thought excursions, keep your eyes moving and noting things. If you are in the country, tell yourself about the different habitats you are passing by or through. "Here's where the swampy bottomland is bordered by an old river bank, and then the maples begin." If you hear a bird song you don't know, try to commit a version of it to memory and look it up later. In the course of the walk, pick up something that intrigues you to draw when you return.

If you are in the city, treat your fellows as fauna and observe attitudes, dramas small and large, variations in

plumage. Note how neighborhoods differ and the kinds of activities going on in each one. If you walk to work, take a different route than you usually do.

When you return, go to your journal and quickly draw, larger than life, two views of the object you brought back from your walk. Under the drawing or somewhere on the page write "Day of. . ." and finish it with a half dozen things you observed that might capture the essence of the day. "Day of low scudding clouds and just emerging willow catkins." "Day of the yellow cat in the alley and the ankle-length red coat."

Then give yourself fifteen minutes to write an account of the walk. As a way of shaking habits, don't make it chronological. Instead of retracing your steps mentally, jump around from place to place, an image here and an image there. This is meant to be your own record, so you don't have to explain everything as though others will have to understand it. Instead of "went down River Park Road past turnoff to Roscoe Merry's house" you can say "Through deep mud in ruts to the place where the sparrow hawk sits." When you are finished writing, try a ten-minute memory drawing, with notes to augment it if you like, of any view from the walk, close-up or far away.

Memory sketches are difficult, but they improve radically with practice. Don't tackle something too complex. Just try to get down the basic arrangement of something you saw. Comments along the side, remarking on the

July 24

Crabbed gestures
of dead baby bats

found on the barn floor.

drawing, can be helpful and revealing: "Hills seemed to loom up larger than this. Just a small puddle can reflect a big chunk of the landscape. Colors are denser when reflected." Try several different versions to see if you can get closer to how it looked to you.

5) LISTING

Lists can serve a multitude of purposes, and take a delightful number of forms. This last exercise will be about lists and include several kinds of lists.

First, take ten minutes and make lists under three headings:

- •Things to accomplish in the next week.
- •Things that kept me from accomplishing all the things I wanted to last week.
- •Steps to take to solve conditions in the second list.

These are pragmatic, problem-solving lists. I believe in using the journal for that kind of activity as well as all the other kinds of writing mentioned so far. By including things that may seem too humdrum you can foil the internal taskmaster, the one who harangues you as you write in your journal, accusing you of fooling around with worthless doodlings when you should be out doing important things. The taskmaster will be assuaged by the efficient lists you make and the way you analyze the "important" things, and leave you alone.

For me, the journal has served for many years as a "life-central." In times of constant travel and change it has been the one place I knew I would find the telephone number I needed, the book I wanted to look up, the idea that so excited me the other day. What you may not realize now is

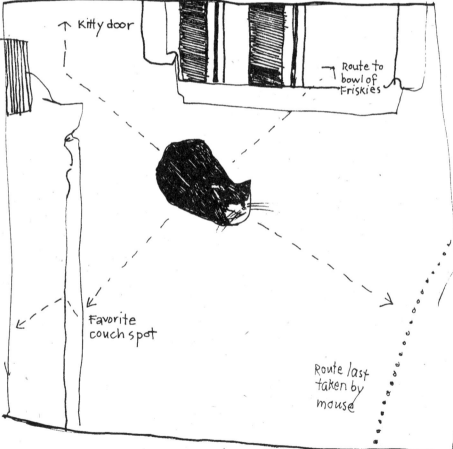

STATIONARY CAT ORIENTATION PLAN

↑ Kitty door

Route to bowl of Friskies

Favorite couch spot

Route last taken by mouse

that the incidental items and casual listings become telling pieces of your history ten years later. The cowboy you met at the local roping and went out with a few times may not get an exhaustive portrait in the actual pages, but there's his number in the back of the book. He's part of your history, like it or not. Errand lists from fifteen years ago are almost like the lists on papyrus found in Egyptian tombs: artifacts that capture a peculiar cross-section of your life. Don't be afraid of compromising the "poetic" nature of your journal by including the debris of daily life.

This list is mentioned in a good book on journal keeping called *The New Diary*. Think over the story of your life, its wanderings, its watersheds, its shining moments. Make a list of chapter headings for an imaginary autobiography (which you may want to begin on when you finish this list) Here is an example from a student of mine:

I. Born in the Heart of the Heartland

II. The Revelation of Reading

III. Losing Sprite

IV. Why is Sixth Grade Still a Mystery?

V. A Failure, then Dan

VI. Real Life Dawns

Try two versions of this, one limited to ten chapters, the other a blockbuster list of twenty or more.

Here's a list that may be more revealing than you think. On the one hand, *Things that Irritate,* on the other *Things that Please.* Be specific. Just the number of things in each list and the ease of coming up with them will provide clues to underlying currents of your life you may not be aware of now.

All these lists can be redone from time to time, and are sure to be entertaining and dramatic in their changes. They

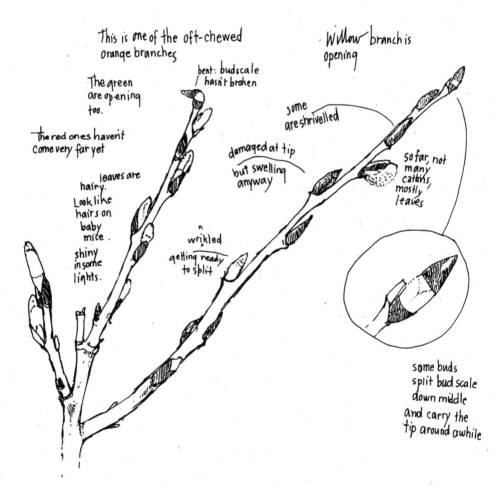

This is one of the oft-chewed orange branches

The green are opening too.

The red ones haven't come very far yet

leaves are hairy.
Look like hairs on baby mice.

shiny in some lights.

bent: budscale / hasn't broken

wrikled
getting ready to split

damaged at tip
but swelling anyway

some are shrivelled

Willow branch is opening

so far, not many catkins, mostly leaves

some buds split bud scale down middle and carry the tip around awhile are easy and don't take much time, so use them to catch up with what can seem like "too much under the bridge" if you haven't written for awhile. A list can take the terror out of facing a maelstrom of projects, responsibilities, problems. They are made manageable, suddenly. You can go after them one by one, and listed, they don't seem to be so many.

Lists are also great memory prods. If I were to start a list of *Great Cafes I Have Spent Time In,* with some details about each, it would produce a volume of its own.

FREEING THE ARTIST WITHIN

here may exist an unknown quality that makes some people able to create extraordinary works of art. Many of the best artists show special early skill, but equally many do not; their drawings at age twelve would not stand out in a random group of talented twelve-year-olds. Nor do all artists who turn out to be "great" (the history books include only a narrow and arbitrary sampling of those) know from the first moment that they want or are destined to become artists. Edgar Degas waffled between a law career and his work as a painter. Van Gogh felt a calling to the church. Reading letters and journals of artists, I am repeatedly struck by the sense of

urgency they mention, a need to respond to something they have seen or felt that moved them. Not an intellectual urge, it seems to come up from below, more closely related to the physical. Van Gogh and Thoreau were both disturbed by the powerful sensations associated with this urge. Artists pursue whatever excites them, groping sometimes, but always tantalized by the chance that next time they'll get it. Georgia O'Keeffe describes the experience: "At the moment I am very annoyed — I have the shapes — on yellow scratch paper — in my mind for over a year — and I cannot see the color for them — I've drawn them again — and again — it is from something I have heard again and again till I hear it in the wind — but I cannot get the color for it — only shapes — None of this makes any sense — but no matter." For Georgia, and for many artists, the senses do not always stay neatly discrete. She uses the analogy of hearing to describe places and colors, and talks about seeing music.

Perhaps the quality, if there is one, that sets some artists apart from others is a visceral response to the world, and their persistence in trying to grapple with it. It's not something acquired later. Rather, it resembles a child's first gestures toward his surroundings and is rooted out of us as we grow up. In those artists it didn't get rooted out, though it may have gone underground for awhile.

It maddens me the way children, when they get to school, begin to show the effects of channelizing immediately. Almost everyone tells me that they adopted a set of symbols to use in their drawings at an early age, and I watch children today  adopting the same rigid set of "replacement images." The tree is two sticks with a ball on top (perhaps with smaller balls for apples). The landscape always appears with the same sun above, or in an upper corner, and the grass along the bottom of the page. A few years later, an even worse lockstep has set in: the boys are drawing their own set of repeated symbols (usually machines, monsters or weapons) and the girls are segregated with theirs (usually horses and/or women in different costumes). I feel sure that the teachers don't tell them to draw those things, and many try to discourage them. The pattern is as mysteriously unbroken as the transmission of kids' rhymes and games.

Perhaps children are reassured by the sameness; certainly they are praised when they finally draw something recognizable. As a youngster, I loved to draw, but stayed trapped in and bored by those restrictions for years. Occasionally irritation would make me try to break out in

some way, but the allure of praise would overrule and I would revert to what I did "well," or try to copy and improve on another girl's chosen subject matter. If only I had had one teacher tell me to go back and look more closely, point me toward observation rather than repetition!

It wasn't until I began my first journal that the hunger for the realness of things, the subtle differences between a red maple and a sugar maple, made me finally try to abandon well-trodden habit ways. That book, a small, private experiment ground, was a perfect place to work in peace toward something new.

Many of you lump all those frustrating days together and just say, "I can't draw." I believe that the visceral response is never really rooted out of anyone, though it may be deeply buried. *Drawing* it out is a learnable skill. It takes persistence, and a willingness to set vanity and ego aside for awhile. If you are willing to try, and ready to abandon old habits, you will make dramatic improvements. It's that simple.

One of the problems with letting go is that few of us have learned to appreciate what an alive and powerful drawing looks like. Most people find themselves admiring the same things they admired in their fourth grade classmate's pictures. As you really begin to draw, and learn what goes into drawing, suddenly you will see that most of what you admired before looks like the imitation it is. Just because the artist was technically accurate in forming the outline of an animal doesn't mean that he invested it with a sense of life, or that you can glimpse any of the artist's discoveries as he drew. The accuracy of photographs only highlights the value of a devoted artist's transcribed vision.

That doesn't mean that accuracy is not something to strive toward, but there are many kinds of accuracy and many ways to get at it. It doesn't work to substitute "artistic" scribbles for the true forms, although scribbles are sometimes the closest you can get to a certain form or feeling. It just means that you are required to invent, reinvent, translate, and be honest.

Perhaps you build up a knowledge of the visual characteristics of trees. That doesn't mean you "do trees" the same way each time you draw. I try to avoid categories, such as "How to draw trees." Isn't that heading right back toward the sun in the corner and the grass at the bottom? The rigidity sets in almost immediately. Possible new connections are thwarted, relationships among things remain hidden. What if one day the bark on the aspen trees started looking to you like the whorls in the creek water? — a notion that offers many rich possibilities. If you had only one way of doing trees, you'd be unlikely to pursue it.

The rest of this chapter will describe elements to keep in mind while you are drawing. Some of them are technical — drawing is a physical act, and you want to preserve the motion of your hand as it travels over the page. So you must be at ease with the tools you are using. Other examples have to do with attitude and intention. I hope they will help you start to form your own language of drawing.

Two warm-up exercises have become standard in many art school drawing programs. They are sure to go against

all of your assumptions of what a drawing should look like, so they are ideal as starting points.

CONTOUR DRAWING

The term contour drawing is at first misleading because it suggests that you will be tracing only the outline shape of your subject. Outline will be involved, but it's only one of many contours you will seek out. Choose a houseplant, or go outside and return with some piece of vegetation that appeals to you, and get a pen to work with. Situate yourself and study your subject for a minute or so. Then choose a starting point on your page or page spread. From here, the direct connection between the eye and the hand takes over. Don't look back at your page at all, and don't raise your hand from it. Begin to let your eye roam over the forms, and allow your hand to follow the path of your eyes, in and out, here and there in no particular order except the way your eye chooses to examine the subject. The drawing itself is not as important as teaching your hand to follow your eye.

You may find yourself returning to areas that intrigue or puzzle you. Don't worry about the overlapping results, or whether you are drawing the leaf in the same place it was last time. Do this kind of drawing slowly and lingeringly, until you have gone over the whole form at least once.

The result may at first embarrass you because it isn't what you think a drawing should be. But look closer. You will be amazed to discover how true to the personality of the forms is the maze of marks you made, though the proportions and positions may be strange or exaggerated. This kind of drawing, though not usually an end in itself, initiates an important vision-link. You will feel its influence as you work at other kinds of drawing.

A modified contour drawing is useful too, as an initial sketch or an under-sketch. To modify it, you can glance back occasionally at the page, or pick up your pencil (pencil is better for an under-drawing) and change places on the drawing. But the basic aim is the same: let your hand feel that it is actually touching the object, knowing its three dimensions, through the investigations of the eye.

GESTURE DRAWING

Another exercise involves a way of drawing that will sharpen your ability to see and glean essentials quickly, a useful skill in the field where animals move and light conditions change. The term is gesture drawing, and applies to you making the gestures of drawing as well as the gesture made by whatever you are looking at.

Everything has its own unique gesture: the table's "tableness," the crows "crowness." When you get to people or animals or things you know well as individuals, the quality gets even more specific, belonging only to him, her, or it. Drawing can find and record the gestures; in fact, such recognition is at the heart of all truly great drawing.

TETON SCIENCE SCHOOL FIELD JOURNAL CLASS

Lake-marsh grass margin   all very orderly, clean edged, simplified
duck raft —mid-lake.

find a sewn-together leaf
(looking for aspen leaf-miners)

clack clack clack clack clack

the loud flying grasshopper lands, shifts rather precisely in the sun, flicks his hind legs. Then goes off again. A display—yellow & black wings. Mating?

read later that certain insects hold body heat at optimum temp by lining up with the sun, or turning broadside to it

inside: little aspenleaf-colored spider with a white egg case bigger than her body.

X 3

Can see little bumps inside egg case — Spiderlings.

legs are translucent body is shiny green, like skin of green apple orange patch at end of abdomen.

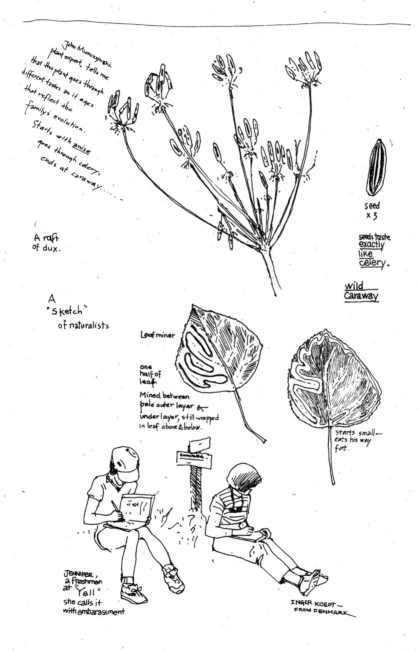

John Mloncezynski, plant expert, tells me that this plant goes through different tastes as it ages that reflect the family's evolution. Starts with <u>anise</u> goes through celery, ends at caraway......

A raft of dux.

seed x 3

seeds taste <u>exactly</u> <u>like</u> <u>celery</u>.

<u>wild</u> <u>Caraway</u>

A "sketch" of naturalists

Leaf miner

one half of leaf.

Mined between pale outer layer & under layer, still wrapped in leaf above & below.

starts small— eats his way fat.

JENNIFER, a freshman at "Yell" she calls it with embarassment

INGER KOEDT — FROM DENMARK

As you start to learn gesture drawing, speed is essential because it is so easy to be led astray by peripheral details. Later, you will be able to get at the same gestures in a more deliberate way, but for now speed will help you cut through to the essential.

You can concentrate on the same plant you used for contour drawing. Make sure, for this exercise, that you have a pen or a pencil that won't balk at loose, fast drawing. For instance, a soft dark pencil would be much better than a tiny drafting pen. Give yourself no more than thirty seconds for each of these drawings and do several, full-page size, from different viewpoints, or choose a detail of the plant or object and do a drawing of just that.

Plunge in with quick marks that try to capture the essential gesture of the plant. Let yourself get physical and make the marks from your shoulders and with your whole arm. Is the plant condensed, knotted, made up of rounded forms? Is it stringy, spiky, lattice-like? With your eyes on the subject, get down the basic and most important information in thirty seconds or less. You may end up with slashes and a heavy horizontal line, but that is what you are after here, a visual shorthand that tracks down the essence.

If you have a bird feeder and binoculars, try some gesture drawings of birds. A page in my journal of drawings of juncos shows some ovals — I was working to get the exact oval shape a junco makes when you are looking at him head-on. There are some scrawled dark and light shapes, my way of learning how the junco's dark head and chest balances against the rest of his body. None of the drawings is anything but a study, though they have some freshness, but I don't forget the lessons I learn about the bird when I draw it. Looking from binoculars to the page and back is tricky and requires practice, but it is a useful ability when you take your journal into the field.

VISUAL EDITING

Soon you will want to work on drawings in your journal that require more time. One of the most important problems you will come up against immediately when you

survey an appealing landscape, an interior, an object, is
"where do I start?" First, as you're looking, make clear to
yourself what attracts you most to the view or the object.
Is it the misty atmosphere of the day rather than the actual
house and rows of trees? If that's so, then try to work your
way into the drawing tackling the problem of atmosphere,
rather than getting bogged down in the angles of the

building or the branches of the trees. It may mean that parts of the house and trees are indistinct or hidden completely. Follow your eyes; there is no rule that says you must dutifully include each branch and window.

It is helpful, again, to make a quick, pale position map using minimal marks, to arrange the basic structure of what you are looking at. In addition, you might partition off several small squares or rectangles and make thumbnail sketches in them, trying slightly different views, making miniature experiments before you start work on the larger drawing.

Once you have begun, two common pitfalls loom. Since so many of our daily activities involve orderly routines, there is a natural tendency to approach a drawing the same way: start in the corner and finish everything step by step till you get to the other side.

Lucy.

As a method, that might work in reading, but it does nothing for art. Remind yourself to move around the drawing, developing several parts of it at once.

One of my art school teachers described it this way: imagine you are beholding a scene nearly obscured by a white fog. As the fog begins to dissipate, figures and objects become visible until by degrees the whole comes forth in clarity. That is a good way to approach a drawing. In a middle stage, only some of the elements may be developed enough to be recognizable. Oddly, some drawings reach their highest level of perfection then. Degas left many of his drawings in this arrested state, and Seurat's drawings certainly ranged from vague to distinct, with all stages having their own beauty and coherence.

The other pitfall is assuming that every square inch of the drawing must be finished to the same degree, that because you elected to concentrate on the gleam of your friend's hair in the sunlight you must also render every leaf and twig of the branch above her. Some of the most exquisite animal studies by naturalists such as J. Fenwick Lansdowne and Charles Tunnicliffe show the animal indicated with economical pen strokes, while one area of it — the head or wing, for example — is brought forth in full detail.

It's your privilege to choose what absorbs you in your subject, and give it more emphasis. In one sense, you are mimicking the way our eyes work. What's in focus is clear and detailed, while peripheral vision records general shapes

and colors. Visual editing will keep you from being exhausted by the thronging elements of a landscape.

On the other hand, some artists make the crowding and multipatterning of a scene the subject of their drawing. The American painter Neil Welliver will fill a canvas with a section of forest floor crisscrossed with lights and shadows and littered with leaves and sticks. He leaves it to us to supply or pick out the underlying pattern. In the National

Gallery in Washington there is a painting by John Singer Sargent called *The Hermit,* another scene of a light-filtering forest. After you have studied it for a moment you realize there is a figure included in it — a man dressed in rags the color of fallen leaves. It is his eyes, rapt and full of visions, that break the camouflage.

EXAMINING NEGATIVE SPACE

The Taoist yin-yang symbol carries a vital message to the artist. If you want to know intimately the apple tree on the hillside, you must know intimately the space that surrounds it. As infants, I am sure we spent as much time looking at the spaces between and the holes through things as we did the things themselves, but, because this activity (in the modern world) has little survival value, it was rooted out of us. The calligrapher knows that the shape inside the letter is as important to attend to as the letter itself.

When you sort out a landscape and begin to draw it, make yourself switch modes often, observing the exact shapes between the branches, and drawing the "negative" shapes instead of the positive.

spruce tree from above

Convention stands between us and our view of the real world. Through my studio window, I look down on a spruce tree. Because I'm looking down on it, its shape is not very tree-like, and as I draw it I have to force myself to put down the shape I *see* instead of substituting a standard symbol for Christmas-tree shape. That is the mystery and

symbol for
spruce tree

challenge of foreshortening. If you were to submerge in a stream and draw a trout nose-to-nose, the trout's face would fill the page and his tail, if you could see it at all, would be distant and tiny. The orderly brain rebels at foreshortened images. Exaggeration on the page can look very strange. Trust your vision. Studying the negative space will help you see foreshortening.

EXPLORING PATTERN AND TEXTURE

Another way of penetrating a complex scene is to study some of the forms, and draw them individually, or even make drawings/diagrams of more difficult shapes. A young spruce tree has a very specific growth pattern and it can be diagramed. Leave out all details and use lines to illustrate the way the branches spiral around the trunk and fan out to fill the open spaces (a tree's task, of course, being to present the most surface area to the sun.) The spruce tree you eventually draw may not be so idealized, but you will have learned something about its nature by analyzing its growth pattern. Or, you may enjoy the pure geometry of the diagram and want to elaborate on that.

To capture the variety in a complex scene, you might start by establishing different textures. There is an unlimited range of marks you can make: antlike strokes, random dot patterns, grid-dot patterns, smooth tones, slashes and scribbles, crosshatching, etc. . . . The key to combining textures is placement. Warring textures will cancel each other out. A drawing can be formed entirely of textures, and need no outlines to be understood.

When you draw, you are setting aside time to admire light and its effects. Color is one of light's masterpieces, but I am assuming most of us will at least begin keeping a journal in black and white media. Tackling all the concerns of color is beyond the scope of this book, but if you are famished for it, here's a suggestion: get colored pencils, or watercolor pencils, and start working them into your drawings. Don't assign green to the trees and brown to the bark: really look. Layer colors. Layer complementary colors like blue and orange. Use small spots of intense brilliant hues. Invent colors by mixing. In short, experiment.

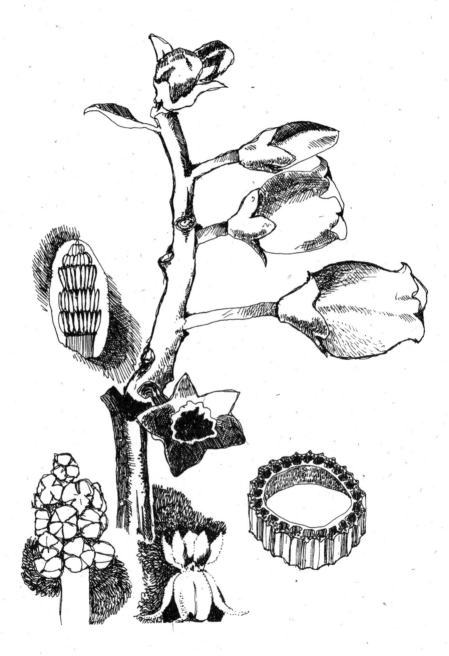

In black and white media, patterns of light and dark will
many times be the dominant theme in what you look at
and draw. Watch the activity of light carefully and don't
substitute prior assumptions for what you see, however
strange it may appear. I remember being taught to look for
the source of light, and then I would know just where to
put the shadow on the other side of the object. That works
well enough with spheres and cones on your table. One
evening years later I sat drawing a distant rampart of
badlands lit by a low-angle sun somewhere behind me.
The same shadow-casting properties were at work here, but
on a scale much more complex and interesting. On the far
left, the vertical ridges revealed no shadows at all. In front
of me, they appeared in half shadow and half light. The far
right end of the rampart was almost all in shadow, with
only a prominence or two lit up. Had I been trying to apply

the formula I had learned, I might have insisted on equal light and shadow across the whole range whether it was there or not.

When you observe the effects of light and shadow, take note of light coming from snow, water, or other reflective surfaces. It can change the pattern of light and shadow in most unusual ways. Allow yourself too, to see the abstract shapes of light and dark. All of nature is abstraction, especially if you are very close up or very far away. A field with walls and a pond is, among other things, composed of shapes: curved bars, ovals, strange polygons. A beautiful dead tree is made up of abstract flowing lines and curves. I have never understood people's objections to "abstract" art, because abstraction is everywhere. Your drawing will benefit from learning to *read* abstract shapes.

Do notice the angle of light and the different kind of shadows that are cast. Is the light brilliant, and are the shadows correspondingly dense? Or is the light more diffuse? As you admire a grove of trees you may notice that there is one combined shadow under it. Even though it is your tendency to want to draw the trunk of each tree because you know it is there, the truth would be better served if you let some trunks stay submerged in the shadow mass. The vase on the table in front of you is white, but because you are seeing it against the brightly lit window it appears in silhouette and is dark. Even trickier: the trunk of a birch tree is bright against the background of brush, but when it comes up against the sky, it's dark. Should you switch in mid-trunk? Emphatically, yes.

Almost unconsciously, when I begin a drawing, I try to identify the brightest piece of illumination before me, as well as the darkest dark. If you don't work with contrast, you are overlooking dramatic possibilities. Don't be afraid of formidable black passages, or areas of such dazzling light that features are invisible in them. And yet, not every drawing needs to be brought up to the highest pitch of contrast. Consult your vision.

What *about* the details? A tree has thousands of leaves. There are many ways to solve this. Instead of drawing every leaf you may want to suggest the shape of some leaves in some places, and let the rest be implied. You may want to cover the whole with a texture that suggests the leaves of that kind of tree. But *are* the leaves important to the whole drawing? Maybe the essential thing is the fact that one clump of trees is very pale, but the grove in the distance is low-slung and dark. What you see could be achieved on the page by using tones alone.

Be aware, in your drawing, of large masses and their shapes, as well as how much of the whole each mass takes up. I'm thinking of a wonderful drawing by Leonardo Da Vinci, of a little copse of birch trees. He positioned them at the top of the sheet, and left the bottom two-thirds blank, giving you the perfect impression of viewing the trees from across a field. In a painting by Gustav Klimt, the foliage of a tree in the foreground takes up about eighty percent of

OATS

the whole picture, with little distant details showing up near the bottom, below and through the foliage. Odd as it sounds, when you see it you know he has been faithful to actual appearance.

These are just suggestions, and they are all things you would discover yourself over the course of many drawings. If any of these concerns begins to come between you and what you are seeing, or you and how good the pen feels on the paper, then forget about them until you get those more basic pleasures back again. Drawing has as much to do with your delight in the shape of the mark you just made on the page as it does with the pleasure you get from the object you look at. In fact, some of the drawings I like best in my journals are the ones that, though not very accurate in portraying the subject, have rich gray tones or bold and graceful pen lines with a life of their own.

Relax and let your attitude be one of curiosity about what you may find out, either about the thing, the drawing, or yourself.

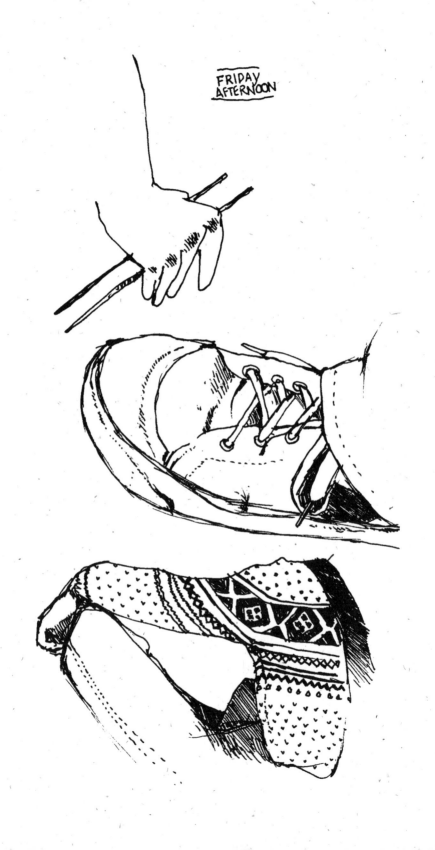

FRIDAY
AFTERNOON

FINDING YOUR OWN VOICE

nly after several years of journal keeping did I even begin to hear my own voice in what I wrote. I had wasted too much energy on proper sentences, assuming that if the grammar were correct the writing would automatically be interesting. Almost the exact opposite was true. My journals from that time, except for the natural history discoveries, which heralded the advent of a new life, are relentlessly dull. At seventeen my personality was nothing if not passionate and willful, but all that came out in the journals were blocks of teenage clichés, insipidities, and stock phrases. I never entertained the idea that writing could reveal, or even shape,

new parts of my emerging self. I stayed locked into writing that couldn't cut through to anything that mattered.

Somewhere in my sophomore year of college, Volume Ten begins to show the influence of an extraordinary professor of sophomore composition. She enlightened and amazed us by insisting that we make the writing our own, whatever that meant. She broke over our heads the idea that as long as our writing remained so sterile and mindless, we would never produce a word that mattered to anyone. "Show, don't tell." It was the first time I heard that exhortation, which rings in my ears sixteen years later with every sentence I write.

During that time I experimented, probably out of boredom and irritation as much as grand plans for improvement, with word play and stream-of-consciousness writing. Those passages are equally full of clichés and slang, but the fact that I was trying to press forward into a new way of examining things was, I see now, a fortunate step.

I read voraciously, copying pages of quotation into my journal, adopting a political and spiritual framework. But words seemed more and more something to play with; whimsy infects many of the entries. The flustered look of the handwriting shows that when I wrote this passage I

Soaking worn feet in Soapstone Lake

thick matted moss, pale green

delicate sedge blooming

dwarf willow

Three by the lake's edge

thought big winds from somewhere were sweeping over me: "But I'm such a scrap pile! Got all manner of seamy sleazo thoughts right next to the profound holy loving ones. Thoughts are thoughts. In a fertile brain all sorts of things ought to sprout. Don't weed 'em. That's like growing all corn, you'll tire the fertile soil out. Let 'em all grow and die. They're all you and none of them are you. YOU watch them from the catbird seat."

It wasn't until some years later that I learned to pare down to the essential, to wait for the sound of my own voice, and use my own eyes. It's still hard to look at the abysmal writing from those early journals, though I am coming to acknowledge that all the steps might have been necessary. Unless I burn those books, I will never be able to turn my back on my history and my failings: they are all right there looking back at me.

The natural complement of writing and drawing provides the breadth you need to capture just what it is that makes a place, a day, or a moment ineffably unique. All of us, even those least comfortable with words, are in truth masters, with thousands of words in our vocabularies ready to secure an arresting sight or a significant moment.

I can think of several ways of writing in your journal that will help you break out of habit patterns. Some of these are solutions to specific problems, and won't suffice for everyday writing. Of course, the best teacher is time: time expended multiplied by time elapsed. These suggestions

are meant to help assure that journal keeping remains
something you like to do, so you'll keep doing it, thus
reaping the benefits of time.

INVITING DIALOGUE

You will find that if you toss a question out into the
journal and listen for a moment, any one of a number of
voices may answer. Our personalities
can be seen as communities of
selves with different attitudes and
different objectives, some primitive
and some civilized, many of them
at odds with each other. Not that
you are in any danger of being
possessed by the voices, or that
listening to them will make them
too real. In fact, allowing the other
selves to speak may mean they
don't resort to more damaging ways of
getting your attention.

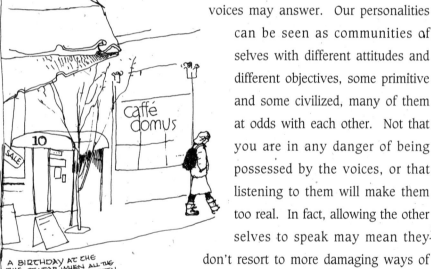

A BIRTHDAY AT THE
TIME OF YEAR WHEN ALL THE
CHRISTMAS GREENERY HAS BEEN
REMOVED.

Sometimes another voice will appear on its own in the
middle of your writing. If your entry has been in first
person, you may see a comment like "who do you think
you are?" or "what are you going to do?" Invite the voice
asking you questions to make a few more comments so you
can see what point of view it represents. Often it will be the
voice of the internal critic, forever trying to belittle your

attempts. You will have to grapple with it eventually, but for now just let the voice speak up.

Draw it into a dialogue by asking it questions. Why does it feel so strongly about the subject? It might be a voice coming from a long-ago event or period in your life, as yet unexamined. It may bring important information. Why is it so angry?

The psychoanalyst Carl Jung believed a balanced personality must contain selves of both sexes, both moving toward maturity. Most of us ignore or mistreat, often unwittingly, Jung said, the self of the opposite sex contained in us. These counter-selves remain undeveloped unless we work to realize them. A man may hear the voice of a pouting thirteen-year-old girl, his anima. Or he may project this inner female outward, finding parts of her in the women he meets. Properly acknowledged, his anima can be a valuable intuitive guide.

A woman may hear the ill-informed opinions of her know-it-all interior male, her animus, who can, if given the right direction, aid her in sound judgment. An eruption into your journal of whining or pouting, or too-rigid opinions may be an indication that your counter-self is speaking. That is the time to inquire of it: "Why do you feel so injured?" "Why are you so desperate to be right?"

big dad, little kid at the Domus.

At times we feel parts of us are asleep, not functioning. By asking questions, we can sometimes wake up the unresponsive part and find out what is causing the silence.

The dialogue can be used even more extensively. As Ira Progoff, in his *intensive journal therapy* suggests, you can carry on a dialogue with your body, or different parts of it. If you are unhappy or blocked about something, the problem often expresses itself through an illness, an injury that won't heal, a chronic pain. Addressing the problem in the journal, asking your lungs why they won't give up a cold, can sometimes trigger a fascinating and valuable conversation.

In dialogues, you can address close friends, parents, dream figures, animals, even parts of the landscape. Give your imagination freedom to take you past the narrow boundaries of *self*. As a result you may develop new empathy for, and identification with, the world.

USING PSYCHIC DISTANCE

Try varying *psychic distance* as you write. At a more remote psychic distance, you use third person, placing yourself in the landscape: "She hesitated in the doorway and wished there was a way to leave, but people were already greeting her." Sometimes this device, especially if it is applied to painful or uncomfortable recollections, can be an immense relief. You are able to give an account of the situation without the sensation of reliving it.

Changing psychic distance can help you visualize futures you hope to bring about. Place yourself days, months, years ahead and bridge the psychic distance so that you feel you are already there. "I am opening a door on a sunny morning and looking into a wooded ravine. Drinking good coffee. I turn to look at the piece of sculpture I completed last night. It is the last in a series that will be shown in the Philadelphia Museum this fall. It looks like a stroke of Chinese calligraphy, made of white painted metal." Athletes use this method, and say it is very effective in influencing the future's actual outcome.

In order to improve your skills of observation, set aside time as often as possible to write long accounts, in the most vivid prose you can command. On a day that seems like any other day, you may find you can remember and comment on so much that you fill three pages without even realizing it. Try giving a full account of your stop at the grocery store; can you re-create your mood and what you were thinking about as well as what you shopped for?

"I dread approaching the meat counter, assuming M. will be working. We haven't spoken in two years, and I'm not sure either of us knows why. So I turn to the row upon row of pickles, so many pickles. Do we really need that many kinds? I still seek the pickle of my dreams, the very astringent one, sliced in strips, on the relish trays of my youth, but I can't tell from the descriptions whether it's any of these. Turning

the corner at the milk I notice that
they have waxed the floor again
and that it looks astonishingly
beautiful and shiny. I'm feeling good
in these sneakers and pleasantly worked-
over from aerobics."

Discovering that your
mind really is active
and curious all day
long can renew your
self-confidence, and
make routine activities
more engaging. ⌐

REFINING YOUR LANGUAGE

Just for practice, edit a long passage, preferably not one
you have just finished. Pretend that you are someone else
reading a stranger's manuscript. Wherever there is an
ambiguity, a clumsiness, a wordiness, try to make it more
simple and direct. When you find a nonfunctional word or
phrase, try to replace it with something more telling, or cut
it out. In John Gardner's book, *The Art of Fiction,* there is a
definition of what the best writing should be. He is
referring to fiction, but it applies equally well to the writing
you do. ". . . the writer sets up a dramatized action in
which we are given the signals that make us 'see' the
setting, characters, and events; that is he does not tell us

Lavender tulips expiring
an extravagant gesture.
Mrs. Arnason's

about them in abstract terms, like an essayist, but gives us images that appeal to our senses — preferably all of them, not just the visual sense — so that we seem to move among the characters, lean with them against the fictional walls, taste the fictional gazpacho, smell the fictional hyacinths."

SEEING YOURSELF IN THE WORLD

I lived in Camden, Maine, when I was twenty-six, during a summer of confusion and emotional bewilderment. In the evenings after work I would change into a summer dress and ride my bike to a cafe by the harbor to drink coffee, sip wine, and sometimes eat a salad. I admired the unmatched

LOBSTER NIGHT wooden chairs and tables and the old lace curtains billowing with evening sea winds. I love to write in crowded places like that cafe — somehow your own solitude is thrown into relief by faces and voices all around you. For the first month I wrote exhaustively about my own situation, its origins and solutions.

A kind of resurfacing occurred then. I started looking around the cafe and saying "Who are these people?" Their accents and clothes and conversations were unlike what I was used to growing up in Ohio and going to college in Indiana. I speculated about how old they were, where they came from, what kind of lives they led. It seemed to me I didn't have enough information about the world to make my way. For the rest of the summer I wrote in the journal about, I suppose, social issues. What is it like to live in a Maine tourist town in the late seventies? Who runs this town, what do they want to see it become? What are the signs of the times here? Is there anything here that reflects the best or the worst of the age? What do the tourists do here, and how do they feel about this place? I had to reach past myself and my limited experience to try to answer those questions. My assessments were, of course, way off much of the time, because I had little information to use in making comparisons. As you proceed

with your narratives, keep in mind questions of this sort
and bring them to bear on what you write.

Because Camden is a small town on an unspoiled coast, I
knew, physically and geologically what its nature was, and
I was already fairly skilled in reading landscapes, as
opposed to human-scapes. But anywhere I go I check
constantly: What kind of ground is this? Glaciated or not?
What do they grow, if anything? Where are the drainages,
where do they go? If you are not in the habit of wondering
about such things, or if you don't know the answers about
your own home range, introduce bioregional thinking into
your way of looking at the world. In the winter of 1981,
CoEvolution Quarterly published a self-scoring test on
basic ecological perception of place. Here are some of the

Evans anchored
at Coombs Island.

questions as they were adapted in the book *Deep Ecology* by Bill Devall and George Sessions.

1. Trace the water you drink from precipitation to tap.
2. How many days till the moon is full?   (Plus or minus a couple of days.)
3. Describe the soil around your home.
4. From what direction do winter storms generally come in your region?
5. Where does your garbage go?
6. How long is the growing season where you live?

7. Name five resident birds and any migratory birds in your area.

8. What primary geological event/ process influenced the land form where you live?

9. From where you are reading this, point north.

10. Were the stars out last night?

To be able to say you really know the place you live, you should be able to answer those questions. They could form the basis of stirring journal entries, and should become a part of your daily consciousness.

SEEING THE PEOPLE AROUND YOU

Creating a verbal portrait in the journal is to me the most difficult, and sometimes the most revealing of tasks. The best portraits combine intensely observed sense impressions with insights into another person's motives, manner, presence. Colette's portraits and sketches stand as some of the most brilliant in any language. Here is one of her descriptions, written late at night on the train, when she was touring with an acting company.

woman with amazing hairdo at Whisper. several men around her

"Another type in our touring company: one of the young actresses. She is married. She brings to the theater the profoundly bourgeois temperament of the 'honest working girl.' I have never seen her idle. From the minute she arrives in a town she stows her valise in a very modest hotel and goes off to the theater to open her trunk, unfold, unpack, mend and hang up her costumes. On stage that evening she earns her living by saying her lines without a fault and without pleasure, goes off at a run, skirts tucked up, to her dressing room, where some sewing she has begun awaits her, and immediately there she is sitting with her work, putting her needle in and out, singing softly to herself . . . she is a worker ant, an honest little ant."

Colette was from rural Burgundy and had little schooling. She says that writing didn't come naturally to her, and that she struggled over every word, rewriting constantly. Though touches like "singing softly to herself" and "without pleasure" sound like inspired choices, they may be the result of many revisions.

To write a portrait of someone closer to you is harder, but the same principle holds. Vary your psychic distance, attempting even to put yourself in the other person's place and see if you can approximate how he or she thinks and speaks. Take down fragments as they come to you over time, then form them into a portrait later, leaving it open for addition and revision.

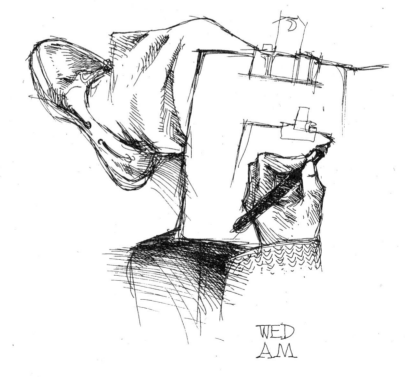

WED
AM

After journal keeping has become a habit, and you've completed a volume or two, an episode of rereading and writing comments is a good idea. It not only provides an opportunity to revel in what you've produced, it offers a chance for a different kind of reckoning. As you reread, ask yourself whether your journal version of the time or event meshes with your memories of it. If you envisioned a future, compare it with what has actually transpired. If you had formed a plan for reaching a goal, was it realistic? Did it help? If not, how did you proceed instead?

Look for repetitive themes. Do they represent a deepening of meaning and understanding, or are they repetitive in a self-damaging way? Identify the best moments. What precipitated them? Is there a thread of continuity among them? Choose some passages you find bring back the spirit of the time most vividly. How do they achieve that?

When you open the journal to write, bring whatever self you are at that moment to the page, as purely as possible. Listen, wait, keep reaching for clarity. Excise the meaningless and habitual. Keep watching.

correct shape
for gull in the water

CHOOSING RAW MATERIALS

have come across only one close-to-perfect hardbound journal, and as far as I know it is no longer available. In England, a company called Laura Ashley designs clothing and home furnishings on an English countryside theme. Among their products, once upon a time, was a blank hardbound book, covered with a handsome fabric of their design. The paper was smooth, so that calligraphy pens and small size drafting pens would glide across it without snagging. But it wasn't coated, as so many smooth papers are: the coating can and does come off and clog pens. It was also heavy and non-absorbent so you could work in wet media without finding that it had bled through

to the other side of the page. And instead of stark,
fluorescent white, the pages were creamy, so ink colors
looked harmonious and interesting on it. If that wasn't
enough, they were the most durable of all the books I have
tried, and at six dollars, reasonably priced. When I last tried
to order one, in 1984, I was told that they had discontinued
the books. I wrote back asking where I might find the
remainder of the stock, intending to order a dozen, but I
never received a reply.

BOOKS

There are two blank books I generally see in art supply
stores. One is made by Pentalic, nicely bound in blue and
black and available in a variety of sizes including an
interesting horizontal shape. I like them fairly well, they
are durable and the paper is heavy, 70 lb. The paper has
just a bit too much tooth, though, for calligraphy pens to
work well on it. Winsor & Newton makes a book in basic
black, but I find its paper a touch too absorbent. I have
been satisfied by the blank books that come with white
canvas bindings, allowing you to paint a design on the
cover if you want.

Look for a paper that has a faint tooth, and one that
absorbs a minimum of ink, otherwise your lines won't be
crisp and you'll be faced with the problem of bleed-through.
Often an art supply store will have a sample book open to
try. If they don't, ask them to open one, explaining that

you are going to have to live with this book for six months and don't want to be stuck with miserable paper.

I once found a clothbound blank book made by Quillmark, the company who makes most of the journals with lined pages you see nowadays. It was a wonderful square shape, but alas, it was filled with something like blotter paper. What can possess these companies, troubling to produce a hardbound book without choosing a workable paper to go inside it?

If you get to New York City, go directly to Kate's Paperie and gaze at the exquisite books, bound and faced with marbled paper, filled with sumptuous pages of the palest tones. If you must have one, be prepared to pay upwards of thirty dollars. If you have a bent for craft, you might begin at the beginning and make your own paper, then learn bookbinding and make your own journals.

natural history near the library

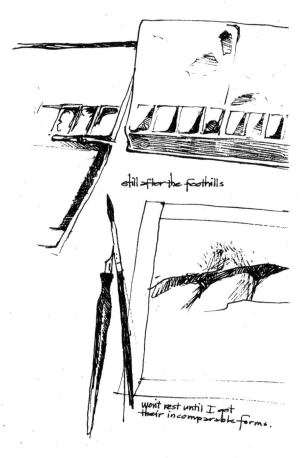

still after the foothills

won't rest until I get
their incomparable forms.

PENS

It's always good to have a selection of drafting pens
around. There is really nothing like the blackness and
precision of a drafting pen line. Discovering them precipitated leaps in my ability both to draw and to letter.
They all leak, except the brand called Rotring, which uses
cartridges. I have the most delicate size practical for use

in a journal, the 3x0; it has never clogged and leaks only
when it is running out of ink. Other drafting pens leak
when they get warm, when they change altitude, or
possibly when there is a magnetic storm on the sun.
Expect a disaster if you take one on a plane with you. The
sizes 0 and 1 are most useful on a daily basis, though they
come in all different nib sizes, from as thin as a mosquito's
leg on up to spaghetti-size. The bigger sizes don't lend
themselves to drawing or normal writing because you have
to hold them almost vertical or they skip.

As miraculous as drafting pens are, they must be handled
with care; you can't get too swift and wild with them or
they will skip and scratch. But there are other pens that
can take over where the drafting pens leave off. I like Pilot
Razor Point pens because they seem to stay sharper than
other felt tips and they have the added quality of being
non-waterproof. You can draw in the field and at your
leisure at home use a brush and water to pull a beautiful
wash from the pen marks. Rotring also makes sketch pens
that offer a much more versatile tip than their drafting pens.
I like to draw and write with the basic Sheaffer fountain
pens, because of the watercolor quality of the ink.
Experiment with ballpoint pens too: a ballpoint handled
correctly can produce an amazing range of tonalities.

Dip pens are harder to carry around, but they can make
the most lively and expressive marks of all the pens. A
holder and a selection of nibs cost only a few dollars.

Include in your collection a crow-quill pen to make the finest, tiniest lines you will ever need. Hunt crow-quills are perfectly adequate. Be sure to use India ink rather than calligraphy or fountain pen ink with dip pens. The latter are too watery for this application and are likely to blot. It's best to use the little eye-dropper cap to fill your dip pen, only a drop or two goes a long way. If there isn't a dropper, take care not to fill the nib too full when you dip it.

PENCILS

If you want to use pencil in your journal, get a selection from hard to soft. I would choose a half dozen: 6H, 4H, 2H, 2B, 4B, 6B. I like to sharpen mine with an exacto knife and a piece of sandpaper, making a long point that remains sharp. Needless to say, you must plan to use a lot of spray fixative on finished drawings, or the pages will smear badly. In the field I use a 4H, for very pale under-sketches, and a 4B for loose, quick, bold drawings. Don't overlook a pencil made by Derwent that can turn into a wash when water is applied to it.

water
insects
by
lamplight

COLORS

Choosing a journal that has heavier paper allows you to experiment with washes and watercolors, though if used extensively on a page you can expect that page to buckle. Touches of wash laid in with watercolor brushes can turn an ordinary sketch into something remarkable. You need a plate, or a palette; the ones with little depressions work best. Make a small pool of ink and have plenty of water at hand. Then you can mix small amounts of ink and water to make the gradations of gray or color you want.

HOLLYHOCKS
CAPUT
AS OF THIS
FROSTY
MORNING

Winsor & Newton makes an exquisite small traveling watercolor set that folds up and carries colors in the dry "half pan" form. You can approximate the same thing with some of the other inexpensive closable palettes available,

STILL GREEN

SEEDS ATTACHED

Seed pods are far more orderly than I expected, with little round flat seeds joined carefully to a central hub. Bud scales pulling back release seeds from hub attachment.

seed with hub-notch
x5

using good tube watercolors squeezed out in small amounts. It is important to get good watercolors, and Winsor & Newton is the best I have found. Children's sets have paints that are too opaque, more like poster colors. Transparent stain in layers is the essence of working with watercolor. Here is a basic selection of colors: alizarin crimson, burnt sienna, burnt umber, raw sienna, new gamboge, cadmium orange, cadmium red, sap green, hooker's green dark, viridian, cerulean blue, ultramarine blue. Investing in a set of Winsor & Newton watercolors like that will cost you over forty dollars.

From England again comes a handy tool: Derwent watercolor pencils, made by Rexel Cumberland. Even without water they work well as colored pencils. Though they are not quite as soft and brilliant as Prismacolor pencils (the best), they have a fine range of colors reflecting the English preference for landscape work — a much better choice of greens. They are easy to carry into the field where you can draw with them, or add color to pen drawings. When you get home, a wet watercolor brush can turn any area of pencil color into a beautifully blended wash.

My favorites are still the Prismacolor pencils. They come in a bewildering array of colors and can be applied in multiple layers to form complex shades. They come in a thick version, and a slimmer one with a slightly harder lead.

Other alternatives for color include colored inks, applied with brush or dip pen. (Don't put them in your drafting pen because some of them contain a varnish.) Winsor & Newton makes a set of them and so does Pelikan. You can buy the Pelikan colors in tiny bottles, just right for the experimenter. Dye-based brilliant watercolors are also available, their hues are stunning and transparent. They are not guaranteed to be lightfast, but that should not be a concern for a journal keeper.

In bigger art supply stores you can find a tool that is made for oriental calligraphy. Its nylon tip is a flexible pointed brush shape, and it has its own ink supply like felt tip pens do. It is ideal to take into the field for brush drawings, and can produce some wild lettering. Pentel, Staedtler-Mars and Tombow all make brush pens in many colors. I have been most satisfied with oriental-made black brush pens because the makers seem to know more about the way a brush should move and feel.

My later volumes have survived the wear and tear of a year's constant handling better because I encased them in a Cordura cover. Most of these have handy spaces for tools and loose papers, so they can be the only thing you carry into the field. Art supply stores also offer light nylon attaches, which provide enough space for a watercolor set, too.

All these suggestions only reflect my own experience — I am always alert for new tools and new ways to use familiar tools. Though conventional journals are limited by size and by the fragility of paper, there is still a world of possibility in the form. Images and language catalyze each other. As your ability to record, invent and design develops, you will use the tools with increasing freedom.

Chunky cottonwood twigs

This is all of one year's growth ?

and this will produce this year's when it unfolds ?

n these days of computer-generated graphics and flawless copies, something hand-made is even more to be prized. Part of the appeal of the kind of journal considered in this book is that every mark in it is made by hand, and that those marks are expressive of a singular personality. We all yearn to make something: the advantage of the journal is that it requires no expensive equipment and no unfamiliar skills. The book, the pen, your hand, your eye; that's all.

In my journals, drawing and writing began as distinctly separate activities, but that boundary has been breaking down over the years. In some cases the drawings, maps, and diagrams especially, become primary message carriers, and the lettering becomes a design element. The interweave of lettering and drawing is a rich ground for play and design. The act of writing itself can become a more expressive tool than you ever imagined.

I use the word *lettering* to distinguish it from *calligraphy*. Though the word calligraphy means nothing more than "beautiful writing," it has come to be associated with certain kinds of pens and certain styles, all of which can be used in the journal. Calligraphy tools and skills, however, are a subject too vast and too diverting to take up in this volume. In contrast, hand lettering is first concerned with how you employ whatever tool you happen to be using, and how you arrange the words on the pages. The beauty and skilled execution of the words and groups of words will be a natural outgrowth of those simple conditions.

I especially enjoy the interplay between the content of the writing and the lettering chosen to express it. Chosen may be the wrong word; as often as not when you begin writing an intuitive choice has been made. The longer you keep a journal, the more extensive will become your library of hands.

ARRANGING THE PAGE

Lettering is a soothing act as well as an aesthetically satisfying one. Forming lines of nicely shaped print is akin to the pleasure knitters and weavers must feel as they watch the beautiful material grow. Following are some ways to imagine how lettering, content, and illustration can combine on a page to form something satisfying on many levels.

•On the left-hand page, a handful of floating pen-and-ink sketches of emerging leaves, and incidental comments about the spring day. A block of print in the corner, bare-bones style of writing, describing the time and place. On the right hand page, fourteen small curved boxes containing thumbnail pen drawings, and tiny comments under/around them.

•Across the two-page spread, an arc of simple, contour-like line drawings of a cat on a pillow, with five words as commentary, the words stretched out like beads on a string.

•Left-hand page, a portrait of two fresh whole wheat loaves; right hand page, a somewhat loaf-shaped map, with written comments out to the sides. Playful writing and commentary anchoring the bottom of the spread.

•Left-hand page, calligraphy practice in the form of three wholly unrelated quotations, a funny juxtaposition in themselves, funnier when seen next to three turtle drawings on the right-hand page. Many different styles of writing and a central core of dark in the one almost-black turtle.

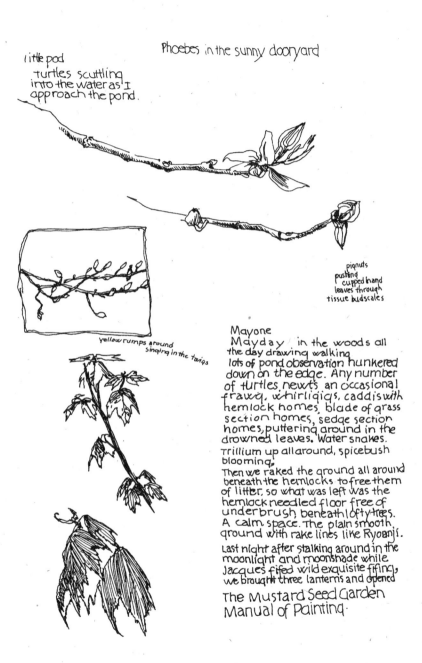

Phoebes in the sunny dooryard

little pod
turtles scuttling
into the water as I
approach the pond.

pignuts
pushing
cupped hand
leaves through
tissue budscales

yellow rumps around
singing in the twigs

Mayone
M a y d a y   in the woods all
the day drawing walking
lots of pond observation hunkered
down on the edge. Any number
of turtles, newts, an occasional
frawg, whirligigs, caddis with
hemlock homes, blade of grass
section homes, sedge section
homes, puttering around in the
drowned leaves. Water snakes.
Trillium up all around, spicebush
blooming,
Then we raked the ground all around
beneath the hemlocks to free them
of litter, so what was left was the
hemlock needled floor free of
underbrush beneath lofty trees.
A calm space. The plain smooth
ground with rake lines like Ryoanji.

Last night after stalking around in the
moonlight and moonshade while
Jacques fifed wild exquisite fifing,
we brought three lanterns and opened

The Mustard Seed Garden
Manual of Painting.

newts drift dangling legs

Jacques fifes from the house

stone walls follow the undulations of rock outcroppings

Turtle returns

mating newts

you have to feel as though there's no hurry

whirligigs and shadows

KEYS A LA MAPLE

whirligigs whirling leave a wake as well as a backwards vibration from their takeoff point

hemlock many turns

out of their sheaths furry like mice

beech leaves heavy on the twigtips

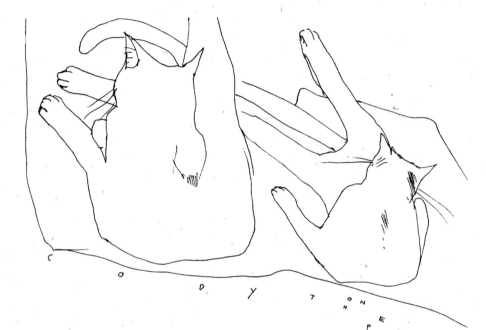

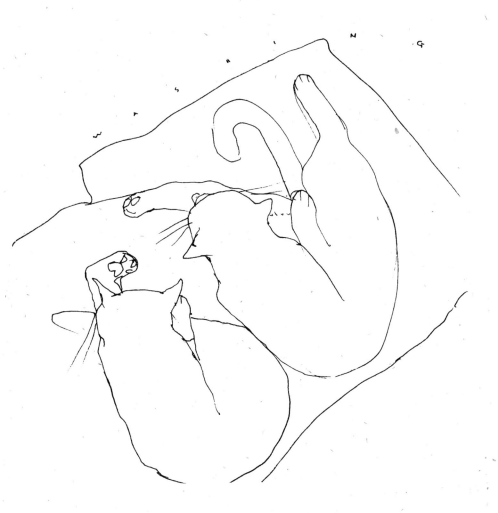

CHICKADEES ARENT
SO BOLD WHEN
THE MAGPIES ARE
AROUND

MAGPIE

LOOKS TOO LIGHT FOR HIS BROAD WINGS
AND LONG TAIL

WHEN HE ALIGHTS WITH THE WIND BEHIND
HIM HE THROWS HIS TAIL STRAIGHT UP FOR
BALANCE
GRACEFUL GESTURE, LIKE A CONDUCTOR'S
BATON.

STREAMLINED LITTLE
RED-BREASTED
NUTHATCH

MICHAEL CALLS
HIM THE MUSKRAT
BIRD?

SPEEDS IN
WHILE FINCHES
ARE EDDYING
AND GETS A
SEED

NOW THE CHINOOK HAS HIT WITH FULL FORCE
OF ITS VELVET PAW — TEMPERATURES
ARE SHOOTING UP AND ICICLE DRIPS
ARE PICKING-UP SPEED.

MAKES ANIMALS EXCITED,
SUPPOSEDLY CAUSES DEPRESSION
IN PEOPLE —

PERHAPS HAS SOMETHING TO DO
WITH MY PROWLING RESTLESSNESS
THIS MORNING

DISSIPATED NOW THAT THE WIND HAS ACTUALLY
ARRIVED. FINCHES ARE JUMPY— GO OFF IN A MASS WHORL IF I SO MUCH AS TURN A PAGE.. FINCH WHORL

PLAYING WITH LETTERFORMS

Once you leave behind the idea that writing needs to start at the top left of the page and continue in horizontal lines until it reaches the bottom, whole new avenues of creativity open before you.

Start right now, with your own normal print. Don't pay any attention to the content of what you are writing at all except make it sentences instead of just words. Print slowly in your neatest hand. Now think roundness. Make your 0-shaped letters into horizontal ovals. Stretch all the letters until the emphasis has shifted entirely to the horizontal.

Now do just the opposite. Stretch your letters vertically, especially the "ascenders" (the tall strokes.) Select out your *Ts* and make them extra tall. That means that you will probably start adding more space between lines of print to allow room for the extra tall letters, so now you also have room for extra long descenders. Write a few more lines in that manner until the pattern of marks becomes evident to you. Now adjust to a less exaggerated stretch and slant all the letters a little to the right to form an italic version.

The effect of any lettering style changes drastically with the weight of the pen you use. An alphabet with very tall ascenders and tiny rounded 0-shaped letters looks elegant and birdlike written with a delicate pen. With a thick-tipped pen it makes an arresting pattern but becomes almost impossible to read. Of course, readability is not always the most important factor. Sometimes the expression of energy or emotion in lettering takes precedence, sometimes simply the rhythm of creating the forms is such a pleasure that legibility becomes secondary.

Size and shape of the letters is only one consideration, but it is the easiest to get hold of initially. As you are changing and working with the letters themselves, you can change the space between the lines, as mentioned above. You can change the edge alignment. For example, quickly draw a small vertical curved line. Using any hand, begin writing, aligning the first letter of each line of print with the curved line on the page, and observe the pattern they make. Print doesn't have to remain horizontal, either. As you are writing along, suddenly decide to bend one of the lines. Make it go down on the end, or up, or put a wave in the

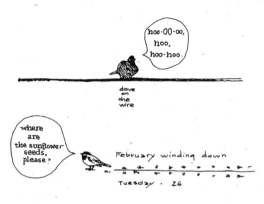

middle. Let the next line of writing follow or respond to that bend in some way. You can bunch lines of writing close on one end and let them splay out on the other like a bouquet. You can enclose a drawing in lettering, you can enclose lettering in a drawing.

And you can vary the length of your lines. What if your lines are horizontal, but each is only five words long? The line breaks may start to sound like the rhythms of a poem to you, and what you are writing may begin to become a poem. Think of blocks or groupings of words. As an exercise when you have more time, make three smallish drawings at random on a page, of anything. Begin your written entry to the right of the first drawing and let the writing filter around the other drawings, interacting with them. The content need not relate to them at all. Let the one restriction be that the entry is readable from start to finish, that it has continuity.

Lettering can become amazingly fluid on a page, bending around and filling unusual spaces. It acts finally as an integral part of the art on the page. The content of the writing will sometimes reflect the spirit of the drawing, sometimes be unrelated and make unexpected contrasts. There is magic in a creative juxtaposition of lettering and art. The ancient Celts knew that when they made the *Book of Kells,* an extraordinary manuscript involving lettering, intricate designs, and tiny color illustrations, in one densely packed whole.

LEARNING CALLIGRAPHY

There is much technique and tradition associated with formal calligraphy. The basic calligraphers' tool, however, the broad-edged pen, is something every journal keeper should have. Eventually, you might want to seek instruction, either from a teacher or from a practice manual. Some of the best books on calligraphy are published by Taplinger, and are available through bookstores. Look for calligraphy pens and nibs in art supply stores. I suggest beginning with a wide felt-tip calligraphy pen — making your letters large at first will help you become aware of their very distinct and specific shapes.

Instructors and manuals place an emphasis on straight lines and consistent lettering, which the journal keeper will,

I hope, take with a grain of salt. Some days it may seem right to fill page after page with impeccably spaced, flowing italic calligraphy, other days you may feel like using boorish block letters in a wild variety of sizes. Absorb the discipline first, then take intelligent liberties with it.

Writer's cramp and maddening impatience will plague your first attempts to develop new hands. Your muscles will adapt quickly, enabling you to fill pages with comely script, but in the beginning confine your practice to half an hour. Even though later you may vary your styles many times on a page, try to be consistent while you are working out a hand. If you have invented a new kind of *E* for the lettering style you are using, repeat it often enough so that it becomes at least somewhat natural. Otherwise you may forget how you arrived at it, and may not hit on it again.

Eventually you will have at your command a number of hands, some you have learned and some you have

gloom and elation
gloom monday disassociated and sick-
and feeling, depressed, angry in object
elation drawing. But out of that, one
gloom moment in the series of distinct
and moments – clogs on cobblestones
elation and a cold wind whipping my
gloom skirt on Moulton St, autumn
gloom loneness, a New England port
gloom city.
elation
elation TUESDAY, elation
elation TUESDAY, elation
Yesterday elation
the day absorbed
by printmaking gloom
so content gloom
so concentrated gloom
ash leaves appearing clear and delicate

THEN DRAWING CLASS the
tension, excitement of an exchange between the
world and the eye becomes almost tangible, audible.
Ed Douglas setting up the intensity and augmenting
it with pointed, cryptic zen pronouncements......
beautiful drawings result and are maps and
artifacts of what we are awash in... Leave
class trembling and awake, wild.
early October 8

invented. Some may not be appropriate or comfortable for long entries, but will add variety and suggest other creative steps. You will find that a "foundational hand," or several, will develop — lettering styles suitable for multipage entries — and that you will shift to others for emphasis, embellishment, or play. Let the texture of drawings suggest lettering styles, and vice versa. Let emotions or physical states influence the way you write and draw. The possibilities are endless, as you've gathered by now.

I hesitate to talk about design. There are countless theories about composition, asymmetry, contrast, and movement. They are all worth knowing about, but perhaps not appropriate to the journal. It's better for the journal to remain a place for improvisation and experiment; having too many design tenets in mind is likely to squelch a sense of ease and play.

In any case, each time you turn to a new page spread in your volume, you're confronted with a chance to design. After hundreds of episodes of arranging space, you will probably discover all the theories of design yourself. I long ago noted that in my journals some of the most beautifully composed pages are the ones with no thought given to design. Chaos and order work out their own arrangements, leaving a trail of vitality on the page.

THE REWARDS

ou have a new book and a couple of pens you like, and you are forging your own ways of working in the journal. You find that you are inventing your own visual language, and you look for new situations and objects to draw, wondering each time what you will make of them. You put something in the book almost every day, whether it is just a note on the progress of the season, or a sentence from a letter you received; or a several-page foray into your own history, something you have never examined before.

The greatest rewards are still ahead, when you have filled a few volumes and begin to know the revelations that can be

LAND TURTLES

WOOD

SPOTTED

PLASTRON:
transverse hinge.

BLANDINGS

expected over the course of many. You are more content with yourself when you are alone, because your life has a history and has proven itself worthy of observation. You watch and listen closely to what other people say, thinking about how you would best describe them. Wherever you travel, you read the ground and also the faces of the people.

Carrying your journal is beginning to be comfortable, working in it is something you look forward to. In fact, if nothing is said in it for several days, you begin to feel at loose ends, a little numbed. The habit of keeping a journal changes the way you absorb experience. Without the rethinking and interpreting that goes on in the book, life dims and becomes less coherent. The journal is a "room of your own," a place of retreat, as well as a way of participating in the life around you.

PERSISTENCE

In the course of the first volume, especially, there will be some pitfalls to avoid, things that will make you want to abandon what you've begun. I have never considered myself very persistent or disciplined. Knowing that, I set up some "rules" for keeping my journal that helped me stick with it. Once it becomes a habit it has its own momentum.

As a first-volume novice you may discover a side of yourself that considers journal keeping a frivolous waste of time. The internal taskmaster, the one that discourages any form of creativity, imagination, and play, is also necessary to us, the goad that makes us keep our lives in repair and moving. But it abuses its authority and tries to root out every activity that doesn't show an immediate tangible result. Journal keeping gains ground for the spirit, brings insight, involvement, understanding, increased attention span and clearer thinking — qualities too nebulous to convince the taskmaster that they're worth the time. "Why aren't you doing the things on this list?" the voice will say, "this must be another form of procrastination."

To assuage it you can introduce the practical into the journal, which is healthy for it anyway. Use it for lists, addresses, recipes, use it to map goals, both short and long term. Use it to take notes at meetings (drawing the people around you in the slow moments). By this gesture toward the practical, the taskmaster will be soothed and you will have in your hands evidence of a unified life, one flexible enough to turn from potato pancakes to the zeitgeist without flinching.

Trying another method, the taskmaster may try to extract from you a promise that if you're going to keep a journal you must make entries in it every day, religiously, preferably at the same time each day. And that each entry must be perfect, flawlessly written, and reflective of a responsible, goal-oriented individual. Nothing will better insure that the journal ends up blank in a desk drawer than to try to keep those promises. When I started mine I decided that I would write in it only if I felt like it, and if it took years to fill it, that would be okay. Even though I didn't feel forced to enter anything in it, I carried it with me everywhere, so that it would become useful at least for the practical things.

Plan on making many brief entries over the course of a

day so that you get used to opening and using the journal.
At first it may seem awkward, but before long you will
accommodate carrying it and even feel "undressed" without
it. Try starting a weather page, where you make a
temperature graph and a brief report of
conditions. Besides bringing you to
the journal daily (you may open it only to
put down the weather, but then end up adding
more) there is something satisfying about
finding a way to acknowledge, briefly, the
continuity of the days.

Morning glory
climbing a
tulip

Tulips have
become
absurdly
long-legged

SHARING YOUR JOURNAL — OR NOT

People will look over your shoulder occasionally if you
happen to be writing or drawing in a public place. You can
discourage the overly nosy by simply saying "I'm taking
notes for a project I am working on," or you can tell them
it's a journal and suggest they keep one themselves. What
I have noticed, and part of what prompted this book, is that
two out of three people will say "I keep one too." or "I
have always wanted to do that." Any of the others who
look askance are probably envious that your life seems
interesting enough to you to write about it.

You should give some thought to the degree of privacy
you want to maintain. There are times that sharing a
journal can be a great delight, to see it inspire others, to
reveal yourself to someone you want to be known by. I let

people read past journals without much hesitation, but I am private about what I am currently working on. From experience, I advise against letting a new love, in the early stages of a relationship, read your life history. Descriptions of other lives and other loves sound all too current to a jealous lover, and you will pay for it forever, if it doesn't destroy the relationship.

I don't believe I have any thoughts or behave in any way that is much different from what anyone else experiences, so I'm not fiercely protective. In some journals I have kept a special section in the back where I enter the most difficult and private thoughts that I would rather no one else see, and that are too painful or embarrassing to want to face on each casual rereading. Many journal keepers are militantly against anyone seeing so much as a page during their lifetimes, which may be the only way for them to assure that the truth will be put down.

FINDING INSPIRATION

As a way to get over dry spells, or to gain new inspiration, read the journals of other writers and artists. I have favorites that I return to again and again, and can never read even a few pages without wanting to go to open my own and try something new.

Thoreau, of course, is at the top of my list. I invested in
the complete set of his journals, in fourteen volumes. He
was less self-conscious in his journal keeping than many
writers, and you marvel at his rich solitude and intimacy
with the countryside. He tried to draw sometimes. I wish I
had been there to encourage him. I like him best when he
stops using nature as a moral example, and yet isn't too
caught up in his meticulous measuring and listing. His
conversational, relaxed, and condensed way of writing
packs much information into a brief passage,
like this one. Listen to the way he keeps
working over the image of the heron, an
equivalent, in words, of contour drawing.

Mouse
Skull

taken intact along with many tiny
bones, from a great horned owl
pellet.
Two times actual size

"As I pushed up the river past Hildreth's, I saw
the blue heron (probably of last Monday) arise
from the shore and disappear with heavily-
flapping wings around a bend ahead; the
greatest of the bitterns with heavily-
undulating wings, low over the water,
seen against the woods, just disappearing,
with a great slate-colored expanse of wing,
suited to the shadows of the stream, a tempered blue
as of the sky and dark water commingled. This is the
aspect under which the Musketaquid might be
represented at this season: a long, smooth lake
reflecting the bare willows and button-bushes, the stubble,
and the wool grass on its tussock, a muskrat cabin or two

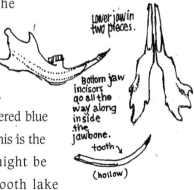

Lower jaw in
two pieces.

Bottom jaw
incisors
go all the
way along
inside
the
jawbone.
tooth
(hollow)

conspicuous on its margin, and a bittern disappearing on undulating wing around a bend."

Gerard Manley Hopkins is best known as a poet. He took orders during his twenties, in 1866, solving the battle in himself, he thought, between the artist and the man of God. Consequently he burned his poems—few survive. For a short time he also kept a journal, an almost deliriously sensuous document that probably, on rereading, increased his inner conflict. He had a fascination with natural phenomena, especially clouds and colors, and coined a word for what happens when a receptive mind sees and appreciates a landscape, a work of art, and is moved by it — *instress.* As a name for the set of qualities that make up the "individually-distinctive form" (the "willowness" of the willow) he used the word *inscape.* Here are passages from his journal. His style is idiosyncratic, but the signs of the watcher are there, vividly.

"At a turn in the road the foam-cuffs in the river, looked down upon, were of the crispest endive spraying. . . .

"At times the valley opened in cirques, amphitheaters, enclosing levels of plain, and the river then ran between flaky flat-fish isles make of cindery lily-white stones. . . .

"I watched the great bushes of foam-water, the textures of branchings and water spandrils which makes them up. At their outsides, nearest the rocks, they gave off showers of drops strung together into little quills which sprang out in fans."

A provincial Frenchwoman, born in 1873, Colette arrived
in Paris with her first husband. At his insistence, she wrote
novels to keep them in beans. To her surprise, writing
turned out to be her life's work. Colette, as far as I know,
never published her journals, but drew from them to
produce the most memorable of memoirs. Following is a
segment of reminiscence about her childhood. She would
travel with her father around the countryside where he
gave "instructive talks," then everyone would gather in the
tavern for a salute of burgundy. She found herself
included.

". . . The session would end in laughter, with slaps on the
back and tall stories bellowed in voices like those of
sheepdogs who sleep out in all seasons — and I would fall
asleep, completely tipsy, my head on the table, lulled by the
friendly tumult. Finally, laborers' brawny arms would pick
me up and deposit me tenderly in the bottom of the

carriage, well swaddled in the red tartan shawl that smelled of orris root and my mother.

"Ten miles, sometimes fifteen, a real expedition under the breathless stars of a winter sky, to the trot of the mare gorged on oats. Are there really people who remain unmoved and never feel their throats tighten with a childish sob when they hear the sound of a trotting horse upon a frozen road, the barks of a hunting fox or the hoot of an owl struck by the light of the passing carriage lamps?"

That's what good writing can be — the seen details, and
an allegiance to the actual. How that passage would have
been diminished if she had said just that "laborers" picked
her up. To a child half asleep, it would be "brawny arms"
that picked her up, and that's how she recalled and reported
the experience.

Colette didn't hold the world at a distance, wasn't looking
for "scenery." She relished each sensation equally without
the usual preference for the pretty or harmonious. She had
a profound awareness of and respect for death, and
understood instinctively its power as part of the essential
cycle.

Robert Phelps, Colette's biographer, says this of her in his
introduction to *Earthly Paradise,* a volume I would press
emphatically upon every journal keeper: "Colette forever
exclaims, 'Regarde! Look!' If her autobiography has any
story it is that of a born watcher.... her deepest instinct, her
readiest reflex, her surest hygiene, was to watch. Advising
a young writer she once said, 'look for a long time at what
pleases you, and longer still at what pains you. . . .' She
knew — perhaps the word is 'trusted' — that to be born
watchful and sentient is a daily miracle, that the 'earthly
paradise' around us is as wondrous an index of heaven as
we shall ever know and that to abide here, even as an
exile, for seven or eight decades, is a blessing — because it
is a chance to watch . . . and to find a better word with
which to secure it for others.

My accustomed seat looking out over the Bowsprit.

"And when we in turn watch Colette watching, we realize that, along with love and work, this is the third great salvation, or form of prayer, that we have been given. For whenever anyone is seriously watching, a form of his lost innocence is restored. It will not last, but during those minutes his self-consciousness is relieved. He is less corrupt. He forgets he is going to die. He is very close to that state of grace for which Colette reserved the word 'pure'."

TAKING COMFORT, BREAKING CYCLES

Keeping a journal effects subtle changes in the keeper, and by doing that quietly changes his life. It's not an

Below deck

undertaking that requires a large time commitment, or any
expensive equipment. If you chip away at it, accepting the
lapses and the dull periods, fighting the feeling of being
overwhelmed by experience that seems too dense and
complicated to write about—it will have a marked effect on
your life. Virginia Woolf, a veteran journal keeper,
imagined her book as "some deep desk," a place to put
anything and every-thing, without forcing it into elaborate
order. She believed that in the rereading process the "loose
drifting material of life" was sorted and refined.

Part of that material will be suffering, which is built into
life, as we all know. Pain, grief, loss, fear, frustration, and

3 · 12

WET BUT PATIENT
PORTLANDERS IN
GREEN MOUNTAIN
COFFEE ROASTERS

THIS STRANGE SLOW
STATE- SURFACING FROM
ANAESTHETIC. TEETH ARE
GONE & SOME PAIN IS SETTING
IN. BUT SMALL PLEASURES CARRY
WEIGHT, LIKE HEATH BAR CRUNCH TO
BREAK MY LONG FAST, AND A GOOD
HOT CUP OF GREEN MOUNTAIN COFFEE;
NOW THE GOOD WINE AT DEWEY'S, THE CRISP
MUSIC, THE FEW QUIET & INTERESTING
PEOPLE AT DEWEY'S TABLES, DISTRIBUTED.

desperation, are as much at the heart as fulfillment. Suffering is intensified by having no outlet, like an electric charge with no pole to arc to. The journal then becomes invaluable. It can take the intolerable edge off mental anguish, can drain away some of its poison. It can have a dramatic effect on depression and other circular thought patterns. Trying to describe the dull hopelessness of depression can alter it, at least temporarily, and often break its hold.

In the book, anger comes out in its true configuration. If you get it out on the page it loses some of its control over you. Grief and loss find a ritual and symbolic resting place; a deeply felt entry can hold and contain them. Fear breaks up into phantoms, and what actually must be faced diminishes when described. This healing power isn't consistent or earthshaking, but it exists and you'll discover it.

MOMENTS OF TRUE WAKEFULNESS

Marcel Proust, in a famous scene from *Remembrance of Things Past,* writes about the taste and smell of a cookie dipped in tea that suddenly brought to life a body of

memory before inaccessible to him. "In that moment all the
flowers in our garden and in M. Swann's park, and the
water-lilies in the Vivonne and the good folk of the village
and their little dwellings and the parish church and the
whole of Combray and of its surroundings, taking their
proper shapes and growing solid, sprang into being, town
and gardens alike, from my cup of tea."

Once you begin to recognize, or choose, the things that
will form the essence of the moment you are living in, and
learn to get them down, your journal entries will have the
same power of calling up for you your own history, with all
its lights and colors, as Proust's cup of tea. That is a joy in
itself. It allows you to view the whole of your life from a
distance, where the patterns and "tune" of it become
distinguishable.

"We must rediscover," said Proust, "that reality from
which we become separated as the formal knowledge we
substitute for it grows in thickness and imperviousness —
that reality which there is grave danger we may die without
having known, and which is simply our life." The journal
is a surprisingly powerful tool to use in carrying out that
rediscovery. It is not meant to be a magnum opus with a
consistent plan. It is an accumulation of moments of true
wakefulness, when you bridge the separation Proust
described. Face to face with an aspen grove, a complex
sky, or an animal's gaze you are able to pierce through the
formal knowledge. By making a record of what you have
seen with a note, a phrase, a sketch, or a lengthy, absorbed
drawing, you make it your own. Next time you turn to
look again, the world will be a degree richer and more
distinct, and you will belong to it more completely.

The
Illuminated
Journal

Watercolors

LOFTY DOES

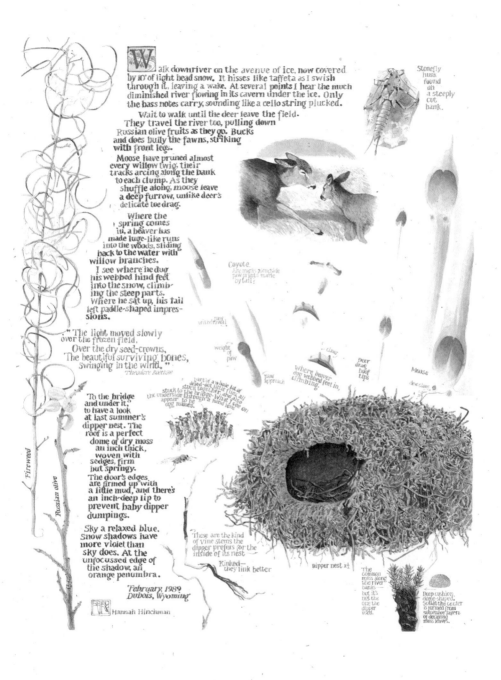

Walk downriver on the avenue of ice, now covered by 10" of light bead snow. It hisses like taffeta as I swish through it, leaving a wake. At several points I hear the much diminished river flowing in its cavern under the ice. Only the bass notes carry, sounding like a cello string plucked.

Wait to walk until the deer leave the field. They travel the river too, pulling down Russian olive fruits as they go. Bucks and does bully the fawns, striking with front legs.

Moose have pruned almost every willow twig, their tracks arcing along the bank to each clump. As they shuffle along, moose leave a deep furrow, unlike deer's delicate toe drag.

Where the spring comes in, a beaver has made luge-like runs into the woods, sliding back to the water with willow branches.

I see where he dug his webbed hind feet into the snow, climbing the steep parts. Where he sat up, his tail left paddle-shaped impressions.

" The light moved slowly over the frozen field. Over the dry seed-crowns, The beautiful surviving bones, Swinging in the wind. "
Theodore Roethke

To the bridge and under it, to have a look at last summer's dipper nest. The roof is a perfect dome of dry moss an inch thick, woven with sedges, firm but springy.
The door's edges are firmed up with a little mud, and there's an inch-deep lip to prevent baby dipper dumpings.

Sky a relaxed blue. Snow shadows have more violet than sky does. At the unfocussed edge of the shadow, an orange penumbra.

February, 1989
Dubois, Wyoming

Hannah Hinchman

Fireweed

Russian olive

Stonefly husk found on a steeply cut bank.

Coyote. Are maple alongside paw prints made by tail?

paw withdrawal

weight of paw

claw

paw approach

where beaver dug webbed feet in, climbing

deer drag hoof tips

Moose dew claw.

part of a whole lot of dried-out little flies, all stuck to the bridge, and also the underside through a hand lens appear to be dog masks.

These are the kind of vine stems the dipper prefers for the inside of its nest.
Kinked— they link better

dipper nest x⅓

The common moss along the river banks— but it's not the one the dipper used.

Deep cushion, dome-shaped. Solid; the center is formed from successive layers of decaying moss leaves.

A STONE BASIN IN EARLY
AUTUMN. A CLEAN-EDGED LAKE IN THE BASIN,
ABOUT TO CLOSE OVER AGAIN. A SMALL WALL WITHIN THE
LARGER ENCLOSURE OF THE BASIN: GLACIER'S LAST STAND.
THE STONES' COLOR RESONATING BECAUSE IT LAYS BESIDE GOLD—
OLIVE GRASSES. THE GOD OF THIS PLACE USES FEW ELEMENTS,
BUT IS PRESENT IN EACH OF THEM. "BELIEVE IN THE SIMPLE
MAGIC OF LIFE, IN SERVICE IN THE UNIVERSE, AND THE MEANING
OF THAT WAITING, THAT ALERTNESS, THAT 'CRANING OF THE NECK'
IN CREATURES WILL DAWN UPON YOU. TO WHATEVER POINT
YOU TURN YOU COME UPON BEING." *Martin Buber. I and Thou*

©89
Hannah Hinchman

"at sunset I walked alone out through the red hills—
—I walked some distance— then climbed quite
high— a place swept clean where the wind blows
between two hills too high to climb unless you
want to work very hard— I didn't want to climb
so high— It was too late— but from where I
stood it seemed I could see all over this world—
—it is so bare— with a sort of age old feeling of
death on it.— still it is warm and soft and I
love it with my skin— and I never meet any—
one out there— it is almost always alone—
and one of the best things I know of—"

GEORGIA O'KEEFFE

...pied another possible
route to the ridge and
conglomerate wall one more time.
blizzard blew in. Ran up against
Stood and watched the squall-veil engulf
Carson Draw, then Byrd, then Dirty Doe, and me.
Snow pellets with beveled edges, collecting in little hollows.
They set off the almost invisible new green tips on mats of
phlox and fringe sage.
I've noticed the earliest growth. Examine a place and day don't seem so stuck
in the dregs of winter. Examine a fringe sage, see leaves from 2 years
ago, curled up grey, and from last year; limp lilac-tan. This spring's new
growth is a foolishly tender green up to the canyon. Now that
> Decide on the right fork this time — proves to have a steep but
passable deer trail all the way to the ridge. Climbing, I put hy
hands on several layers of Wild River formation — red, pink
me pause. They are river-smoothed, full of cobbles. The cobbles make
and gray; faceted, rounded, full of cobbles. The cobbles make
granite with some oddities thrown in. They've been motionless
in these sediments, far from water, for sixty-five million years. Motionless
while Yellowstone volcanoes laid down thousands of feet of lava, while
the glacier pushed boulders to within a half mile of this canyon,
yet once they made the journey down from newly-formed mountains,
part of some lively torrent, carried along in floods...

> Hid in a limber pine shelter to eat lunch. Heavy snow,
then the sun out — blue sky still filled with flakes.
Shadows of flakes on trunk.

> Overland to narrowest arm of Byrd Draw, still
draining a rivulet of snowmelt. Tiny quartz - piece
pyramid: rill had carried hundreds of quartz
grains about this size over a lip and piled
them in a multicolored cone 3 inches tall.

> Walking out. Liberated cobbles in the
wash are strong presences, going
somewhere, in circulation again.

Northwest Wyoming
Early April 1989

"Come quickly
Spring!
Come and lift us
to our ends,
to blossom,
bring us
to our summer,
we who are
winter-weary
in the winter
of the world.
Come and
soften the
willow buds
till they are
puffed and
furred then
blow them
over with gold.
Let the darkness
be warmed,
warmed through
to a ruddy
violet,
incipient purpling
towards summer
in the heart of man."

— D.H. Lawrence

Bunches of
frigida

feather
out minutely
from mat
smell is like
sky thrown
distant
gray-green tundra

Cottonwood leaves emerging

Aspen Catkins
1. Just breaking sheaths,
fur condensed

2. Extending, flower parts
being revealed

3. Fully extended
fur and bracts dropping

Farther up Wagon Box Draw, skirting courting Kestrels. Decide to wander up a side canyon: the approaching storm seems to be moving only very slowly from the east, maybe generating one of East Fork's fabled freak downpours. I have time, unless something whips up in the west.

It's a modest little canyon, a series of rocky terraces thick with vetch and lupines, with a singing rock wren every 50 feet or so. Wren Garden Canyon. Have yet to locate a nest; want to see the pavement of small flat stones they build, leading to the nest crevice.

Close your eyes and hear the song of the light:

Noon takes shelter in your inner ear

Close your eyes and open them:

There is nobody not even yourself

Whatever is not stone is light

OCTAVIO PAZ

The canyon opens out into sunny grassy slopes with the wash curving away, enticingly towards the storm. Golden Eagle ahead, close to the ground. Shadow, as it traverses sagebrush, rocks and grass, is more animated than steady-winged eagle himself.

WHITE-THROATED SWIFTS IN PURSUIT OF EACH OTHER, GIVING THEIR SKRITCHETY CALLS.

Perched on a bald, eroded hillock trying to paint a high-contrast badlands buttress.

Someone else has considered this a good vantage point – several small vertebrae and a little broken femur (?) were left right on top, where they're casting dramatic shadows.

KESTRELS REST TOGETHER AFTER MATING.

TWO CANYON VIEWS......

#11 Hannah Hinchman
© 1989

Clearly the glacier plowed through this valley, in fact it looks so recent you think it might be just ahead, around the bend. And it is, really. Of course that glacier is small and hiding out on the Continental Divide, but it will be ready to move again when the time comes.

In Jakey's Fork the glacier plucked, polished and left huge granite 'erratics' all over the place, having transported them from the core of the Wind River Range. These immense boulders sit around on terraces of scoured sandstone looking like

The exposures of sandstone and limestone have a zen-garden look that I love. Junipers and limber pines seem carefully planted and pruned for graceful shapes. Beds of sage, penstemon, globe mallow and stonecrop flourish in the sandy spots. Orange and green lichens, older than most of the trees, color boulders and outcrops alike. All very spare, severe, pared down.

There's an unexpected crop of cicadas, the buzz-saw kind; they sing during the day's hottest hours and magnify the heat. I find their husks all over, neatly split along the back, clear hemispheres like submarine windows where the eyes were.

JAKEY'S FORK
June 1989

penstemon

Cicada: push wings backward, vestigial like front legs

polite foreign tourists.

globe mallow

stonecrop succulent

Hannah Hinchman
©1989 #14

Wandering towards the sandstone ledge-gardens on an unruffled June morning, looking at illuminated junipers. There are dead juniper stubs too, handsomely blackened. I like to just sit on a glacial boulder, waiting for animal life to resume around me and admiring the details of these ledges.

Nearby there's a fine conical hill of quartz-mining ants, lit up like a view of Mt. Fuji. These artistically exacting ants cover their hill with a smooth layer of almost uniform quartz and granite grains. If you so much as push a few grains around on the hill, the ants hurry out to redistribute them properly. You can see how as good building material they're often found on hills like these. Beads would strike them as good building material. I see splendidly composed heads on the ground I see splendidly composed patterns and delicate flowers against lichen-covered rocks. The shapes, patterns and colors are tapestry-like in their intricacy.

Everywhere I look on these hills I see botanical still-lifes. Cushion plants and silvery-gray leaves cluster against lichen-covered rocks. The shapes, patterns and colors are tapestry-like in their intricacy.

I hear green-tailed towhees, juniper singing color on their backs, singing from several perches.

Nighthawks are back, the quintessential summer birds. I pick out the syncopated flight pattern the male uses just before his wing-rushing plunge.

The CM Ranch guards access to this valley. Here comes its manager and a friend on horseback. They hail me and tell me to put them in my picture...

JAKEY'S FORK
JUNE 1989

Hannah Hinchman
© 1989
#15

A.m. selected quartz & granite grains

actual size

Frogs fill every little flooded hummock hole
bordering the spring creeks.
As froagie is to handle as butterflies.

floating
and
holding onto
a rush stem...
back legs
semi-transparent

these little frogs, when floating, are
the perfect image of buoyant relaxation,
to be thought of when one can't sleep.

evening grosbeaks keep up a steady
rain of halls as they crack out juniper berries

spring
pool
behind
Madelaine's
cabin

the
little
gate to
creek
and
pasture

O sprey spirit stands guard over osprey nest at the head of Torrey Lake. Steep, bouldery moraine rises from there. I find I'm standing still, staring at an ordinary moraine hillside, suddenly struck with its subtle, quilt-like pattern of colors. Then the rocks burst into song — somewhere there's a rock wren — spy him running like a mouse across a green-lichened boulder.

Woodyard Draw's old forest closes in and for awhile I just climb, aware of the smell of dawn-chilled earth. Torrey Rim and its immense grassy bowl are filled with sun, bluebirds out in the open and sapsuckers calling from the borders of spruce-fir forest... The view when I turn around... The view when I turn around: many-layered. 1) Sandstone talus slope that forms one wall of the Torrey Rim bowl. 2) Smooth grassy Wind River Range foothills. 3) Moraine on the far side of Torrey Valley — a little of Julia Lake showing. 4) Badlands across the River, Mason Draw draining them. 5) Rubbly, treeless hills (Spring Mountain). 6) Timbered Absaroka foothills. 7) Snowy Absaroka plateaus.

Bighorn Sheep are grazing on the rim, rams and ewes together. I walk among them and settle in to draw and eat lunch. They settle in, too — lie down, doze in the sun.

Find rock wren at left.

chsing chsing chsing chsing Chubby Chubby Chubby Cho-dee Cho-dee — Rock Wren Song

...ers that affect the whole moraine-scape

close up of lichen on...

When despair for the world grows in me
And I wake in the night at the least sound
In fear of what my life and my children's lives may be,
I go and lie down where the wood drake
Rests in his beauty on the water, and the great heron feeds.

I come into the peace of wild things
Who do not tax their lives with forethought
Of grief. I come into the presence of still water.
And I feel above me the day-blind stars
Waiting with their light. For a time
I rest in the grace of the world, and am free.

— Wendell Berry

Torrey Valley
&
Torrey Rim
May, 1990

Hannah Hinchman

Limber Pine

Dippers

Summer solstice evening walk. Many birds have fallen silent. When I watch the pair of dippers working the shallows its clear from their air of concentration and haste that they're desperately busy. Kestrels, mating noisily all day long a few weeks ago, move quietly now. Watch a harried sapsucker fly impatiently from tree to tree checking sap traps and flycatching in between. Formerly invisible spider webs suddenly stand out, choked with dandelion seeds and aspen fluff; spiders have abandoned them. Every spruce, fir and pine is starred with new growth. Spruce buds in threes shedding papery sheaths to reveal tightly-packed tender needles, soon to extend into complete branchlets.

At dusk the cool air flowing downhill "ponds" in the low spots, fragrant with a musty antique-wood smell. Along the river it's the spicy jasmine scent of silverberry.

NIGHTHAWKS

Spruce shedding sheath

WIND RIVER June 1989

Rain-washed Russian olive or silverberry

Hannah Hinchman © 1989 #13

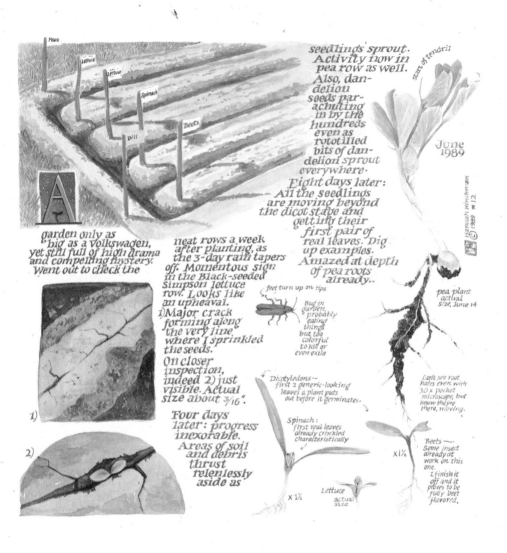

seedlings sprout. Activity now in pea row as well. Also, dandelion seeds parachuting in by the hundreds even as rototilled bits of dandelion sprout everywhere.

start of tendril

June 1989

Hannah Hinchman © 1989 #12

Eight days later: All the seedlings are moving beyond the dicot stage and getting their first pair of real leaves. Dig up examples. Amazed at depth of pea roots already..

A garden only as big as a Volkswagen, yet still full of high drama and compelling mystery. Went out to check the

neat rows a week after planting, as the 3-day rain tapers off. Momentous sign in the Black-seeded Simpson lettuce row. Looks like an upheaval. 1) Major crack forming along the very line where I sprinkled the seeds.

On closer inspection, indeed 2) just visible. Actual size about 3/16".

Four days later: progress inexorable. Areas of soil and debris thrust relentlessly aside as

feet turn up on tips

Bug in garden, probably eating things but too colorful to kill or even exile

Dicotyledons—first 2 generic-looking leaves a plant puts out before it germinates.

Spinach: first real leaves already crinkled characteristically

x 1½

Lettuce actual size

x 1½

pea plant actual size, June 14

Can see root hairs even with 30 x pocket microscope, but know they're there, moving.

Beets — Some insect already at work on this one. I finish it off and it proves to be fully beet flavored.

1)

2)

1.

2.

3.

4.

Actual Size

CRESS in the WATERCRESS CABIN pool
Brought home, examined in a
tall glass vase, it suddenly reveals
a wealth of life.

1. Mosquito wigglers
   looping & relooping
2. Tiny Snail
3. Active larva
   *climbing around in the
   leaves. Air bubbles
   attach to his head,
   floating him off his
   perch & he uses his
   front legs to dislodge
   them, with an
   exasperated
   gesture.*
4. Caddisfly larva
   *in hollow-stem home,
   bumbling along the
   bottom.*

CRESS *and* FROST CRYSTALS

FALL CREEK ROAD

Hannah Hinchman lives in Jackson Hole, Wyoming, where she is a freelance artist, writer, illustrator, graphic designer, teacher and calligrapher. She attended Western College in Oxford, Ohio, until it closed, then Earlham College in Indiana until she ran out of money, finally getting a BFA ten years later from the Portland School of Art in Maine.

Her work has appeared most recently in *Sisters of the Earth,* edited by Lorraine Anderson, and in *Sierra* magazine. She teaches field journal workshops for the Yellowstone Institute, the Snake River Institute, and the Teton Science School in summer.

All the black and white drawings in this book were taken from Hannah's over 20 years of journals. Bruce Cameron photo.